Succeed in
IELTS
Reading &
Vocabulary

TELEPHONE

Andrew Betsis
Lawrence Mamas

GlobalELT
ENGLISH LANGUAGE TEACHING BOOKS

IELTS FORMAT

Academic
For entry to undergraduate or postgraduate studies or for professional reasons.

General Training
For entry to vocational or training programmes not at degree level; for admission to secondary school and for immigration purposes.

The test Modules are taken in the following order:

MODULE	QUESTIONS	TIME	QUESTION TYPES
Listening	4 sections, 40 items	*approximately 30 minutes*	multiple choice, short-answer questions, sentence completion, notes, form, table, summary, flow-chart completion, labelling a diagram/map/plan, classification, matching
Academic Reading	3 Sections, 40 items	*60 minutes*	multiple choice, short-answer questions, sentence completion, notes, form, table, summary, flow-chart completion, labelling a diagram/map/plan, classification, matching, choosing suitable paragraph headings, identification of author's views, - yes, no, not given, - true, false, not given questions
General Training Reading	3 sections, 40 items	*60 minutes*	
Academic Writing	2 tasks	*60 minutes*	**Task 1** (150 Words - 20 minutes) Candidates have to look at a diagram, chart, or graph and present the information in their own words. **Task 2** (250 Words - 40 minutes) Candidates have to present a solution to a problem or present and justify an opinion.
General Training Writing	2 tasks	*60 minutes*	**Task 1** (150 Words - 20 minutes) Candidates have to respond to a problem with a letter asking for information. **Task 2** (250 Words - 40 minutes) Candidates have to present a solution to a problem or present and justify an opinion.
Speaking		*11 to 14 minutes*	It consists of three parts; **Part 1** - Introduction and interview **Part 2** - Long turn **Part 3** - Discussion
		Total Test Time *2 hours 44 minutes*	

Contents

Published by GLOBAL ELT LTD
www.globalelt.co.uk
Copyright © GLOBAL ELT LTD, 2012

Contributors:
Sean Haughton, Christina Oliver and Linda Collins

Every effort has been made to trace the copyright holders and we apologize in advance for any unintentional omission.
We will be happy to insert the appropriate acknowledgements in any subsequent editions.

British Library Cataloguing-in-Publication Data

A catalogue record of this book is available from the British Library.

● Succeed in IELTS Reading & Vocabulary - Student's Book - ISBN: 978-1-904663-88-1
● Succeed in IELTS Reading & Vocabulary - Teacher's Book - ISBN: 978-1-904663-89-8
● Succeed in IELTS Reading & Vocabulary - Self-Study Edition - ISBN: 978-1-904663-90-4

The authors and publishers wish to acknowledge the following use of material:
The photos in Units 1- 10 © Ingram Publishing Image Library - © www.123rf.com Image Library

Map of the book

Unit Title	Reading 1	IELTS Exam Task	Vocabulary	Reading 2	IELTS Exam Task
Unit 1 21st Century Lifestyle	Living a Long and Prosperous life	IELTS Exam Task -Multiple Choice EXAM STRATEGY: Skimming & Scanning	Life in the Fast Lane	Back To Basics	IELTS Exam Task Flow-chart
Unit 2 Career & Life Choices	Art at the Olympic Games	IELTS Exam Task - Multiple Choice - Short-answer questions - Matching information EXAM STRATEGY: Classification	American Abstract Expressionism	The Louvre	IELTS Exam Task Diagram label completion
Unit 3 Around the World	Theme Holidays	IELTS Exam Task - Matching headings - Short-answer questions EXAM STRATEGY: Choosing Headings for Paragraphs or Sections of a Text: Identification of writer's views /claims or information in the text	The new space tourists	The new space tourists	IELTS Exam Task - Note completion - Diagram label completion
Unit 4 The Animal Kingdom	Take a walk on the wild side	IELTS Exam Task - Matching information - Sentence Completion EXAM STRATEGY: Locating Information Skimming & Scanning	Wildlife in danger	Modern day dinosaurs	IELTS Exam Task - Chart completion
Unit 5 A Place to Call Home	The Ins and Outs of Real Estate	IELTS Exam Task - Matching information - Notes / Table / Summary/ Flow-chart Completion	Hotline set up to deal with difficult neighbours	Ice Houses	IELTS Exam Task - Diagram label completion
Unit 6 Education for All	In fine voice - the stress of teaching	IELTS Exam Task - Matching information - Sentence Completion	Beating the playground Blues	The Irish Education System	IELTS Exam Task - Diagram label completion
Unit 7 The Earth under Threat	Global warming: the final verdict	IELTS Exam Task - Short-answer questions - True / False /Not given	Ecosystems fight back	The Perfect Storm	IELTS Exam Task - Diagram label completion
Unit 8 Technological Advances	The Mechanical Insect	IELTS Exam Task - Multiple Choice - Matching information - Short-answer questions	Einstein - a man of strong principles	Advances in Lighting Technology	IELTS Exam Task - Chart completion
Unit 9 A life of Crime	A life of crime is bad for your health	IELTS Exam Task - Matching headings - Diagram label completion - Summary Completion	Is there a lawbreaker in us all?	The Question of Free Will	IELTS Exam Task - Multiple Choice
Unit 10 Health and Welfare	Boiling point - the pressures of modern life	IELTS Exam Task - Multiple Choice - Matching information - Short-answer questions	A Dying Continent	Crisis Point Reading 3 And The Blind Shall See	IELTS Exam Task - Chart completion

IELTS
EXAM GUIDE

READING SECTION

OVERVIEW

What's it all about?

- Reading Passage 1 features a TEXT, USUALLY FACTUAL OR DESCRIPTIVE, OF UP TO 900 WORDS. Typically, you can expect to see BETWEEN TWO AND THREE TASKS, with A TOTAL OF 13 QUESTIONS. Passage 1 will usually be slightly easier than Passages 2 and 3.

- Reading Passage 2 will also feature A TEXT OF UP TO 900 WORDS. There will be TWO TO THREE TASKS AND EITHER 13 OR 14 QUESTIONS in total. Passage 2 will typically be more challenging than Passage 1.

- Reading Passage 3 will feature A TEXT OF UP TO 950 WORDS. There will again be TWO OR THREE TASKS WITH A TOTAL OF 13 OR 14 QUESTIONS. Passage 3 will normally be more challenging than Passages 1 and 2.

What's it testing?

Your understanding of texts which could be included in an academic course is being tested, as well as your ability to follow an argument and opinions. You will be required to employ a range of reading skills including *reading for main ideas* (gist-read) and *reading for detail*, in addition to understanding the structure of a text at both sentence and paragraph level.

What types of tasks can I be asked to complete?

The Reading Paper has a variety of different task types. We will look at each one of these in detail later, but, for now, here is a list of all the tasks which can appear:

(i) True/False/Not given
(ii) Flow-chart completion
(iii) Multiple choice
(iv) Summary completion (type 1)
(v) Summary completion (type 2)
(vi) Short-answer questions
(vii) Yes/No/Not given

(viii) Matching headings
(ix) Matching sentence endings
(x) Matching information/names
(xi) Table/Note/Sentence completion
(xii) Locating information
(xiii) Diagram labelling

TASK INFORMATION: TRUE/FALSE/NOT GIVEN

This task requires you to compare the information presented in a series of statements with the information given in the text and decide if the two correspond.

You must:

(i) read the statements (which follow the order of the information presented in the text).
(ii) scan the text to locate the information you require to compare with the sentences.
(iii) decide whether the information in each statement agrees with the text (True), contradicts the text (False), or is not covered in the text (Not given).

Sample Reading Passage 1.1

In order to examine the different task types individually, this text has been broken up into sections. Read the first section now and then answer the questions which follow.

A brief history of Punk

The punk subculture evolved simultaneously in the mid-70s in the U.S. and Britain. Its inspiration came in many forms; from literature and film, art, music and from earlier subcultures. It drew on the work of Charles Dickens and his unromantic depictions of disenfranchised youths being exploited by the upper-middle class. George Orwell's *Nineteen Eighty-Four* was another unlikely source of inspiration. Films like *A Clockwork Orange* had a part to play in the development of the unique punk style, too. Andy Warhol's pop art was viewed in many ways as iconic early punk, and, in fact, his Factory studio was hugely influential in the development of the New York punk scene. Musically, punk was a reactionary movement, rebelling against what it saw as the utter superficiality of 'disco' music and the style-over-substance approach of heavy metal and progressive rock bands whose performances punk musicians hardly rated. Punk, then, embraced a simpler, more down-to-earth do-it-yourself attitude; punk artists were not trying to achieve musical perfection or trick the audience into mistaking their stage effects and bombastic tones for something special.

Punk removed the cloak of pretension and offered raw, uncensored beats; a sort of street-smart, working-class genre that had not been seen before.

Stylistically, the punks were influenced by the hippie counter-culture of the 60s; bright colours, loose clothes, unkempt appearances and carefree attitudes. The difference being though that they weren't preaching peace and happiness, but a much more aggressive message - a challenge to all authority figures, who the punks viewed with utter contempt. 'All you need is love', the hippies may have proclaimed, but, to the punks, this was soppy nonsense. Their message had more violent undertones and the movement became associated with anarchic politics, protest and civil disobedience and extreme forms of socialism. Biker-gang dress became increasingly popular, too, amongst followers, and jeans, T-shirts, chains, leather jackets and army-style boots intermingled with the hippie flowers and bright colours.

Attitude wise, the punks arguably had a lot more in common with the bikers than they had with the hippie movement, so perhaps this subtle style transformation was quite apt.

Questions 1-7

Do the following statements agree with the information given in Sample Reading Passage 1.1?
In boxes 1-7 on your answer sheet, write

		T	F	NG
TRUE	*if the statement agrees with the information*			
FALSE	*if the statement contradicts the information*			
NOT GIVEN	*if there is no information on this*			

1 In his work, Charles Dickens took advantage of upper-middle class youths. ☐ ☐ ☐

2 Andy Warhol became a very influential performer of the New York music scene. ☐ ☐ ☐

3 Punk artists regarded disco music as quite shallow. ☐ ☐ ☐

4 Punk artists were not overly concerned with their technical proficiency as artists. ☐ ☐ ☐

5 Punks and hippies had more in common stylistically than ideologically. ☐ ☐ ☐

6 The punk genre became synonymous with anti-establishment activities. ☐ ☐ ☐

7 Many bikers embraced punk culture. ☐ ☐ ☐

Remember:
- You will always be able to find the answer by reading the text; you are not expected to use your own knowledge.
- There is always at least one TRUE, one FALSE and one NOT GIVEN answer.
- You should scan the text for key words to help you locate the information you need and then read the relevant section carefully to see if it corresponds with the information in the statement.

Method:
(i) Look at the title of the text and the information below it to get an idea of what it might be about (this helps you to contextualise the questions and gets your mind processing any background knowledge you have to help you predict and/or absorb the content of the passage more easily).

(ii) Read the text quickly to get an idea of what it is about; don't dwell on words you do not understand (this is called *reading for gist*).

(iii) Look at the questions and underline the key words.

(iv) Use the key words to help you find where in the passage the information related to question 1 is found, then read this information carefully to help you decide your answer.

(v) Repeat for the remaining questions.

TASK INFORMATION: FLOW-CHART COMPLETION

This task requires you to understand a description of a process or sequence of events. You must:
(i) scan the text to locate specific information - use the words in the flow-chart to help you.
(ii) find the required number of words and/or a number in the text for each question and copy them into the relevant gap.

Remember:
- All the information you need to complete the flow-chart will be contained in the text, but it may not necessarily be in the same order as it is asked for in the flow-chart.
- Always check the instructions and make sure you write the correct number of words in each gap.
- Parts of the flow-chart that do not have a gap can be used to help you locate the information in the text needed to answer the next question.
- The flow-chart may relate to information in all or part of the passage.
- You cannot change the word(s), or the form of the word(s), you copy in any way; they must be exactly as they appear in the text.

Method:
(i) Look at the instructions and make a mental note of how many words you must write.

(ii) Read the heading of the flow-chart; this will help you find the part of the text you need.

(iii) Read the flow-chart and underline the key words in each question.

(iv) Decide what kind(s) of word(s) you may need to fill each gap (i.e. noun, verb, adjective etc.).

(v) Scan the text to find the part(s) you need and then read it carefully.

(vi) Underline the word(s) in the text which fit(s) the gap.

(vii) Copy them into the gap and read the sentence to make sure that it makes sense.

Sample Reading Passage 1.2

In order to examine the different task types individually, this text has been broken up into sections. Read the second section now and then answer the questions which follow.

A brief history of Punk cont.

It is thought that punk became popularised as a youth movement for much the same reasons in both New York and London. Many working class youths felt socially excluded in the era of post-war consensus politics. They had few opportunities and felt isolated and left behind. Punk was a way to express their frustration and anger at the rest of the world, and their dislike of what was becoming of the mainstream. In New York, the 'punk' label was first used to describe bands that played regularly at the CBGB and Max's Kansas City clubs. Regulars included the likes of The Ramones, Blondie and Talking Heads. In 1976, *Punk Magazine* first appeared and punk music was officially born.

Though New York had been its birthplace, and influential in determining the early sound of punk, the London punk scene would come to define this subculture. Malcolm McLaren and Vivien Westwood opened up their punk-clothing store there in 1975, producing radical new outfits which were bold, colourful and in-your-face – encapsulating the essence of punk. It wasn't long before punk had a cult following in London. Bands like the Pistols were also coming on to the scene at the same time - London had an appetite for rebellion and soon the punk movement really took off. Inspired by the Pistols, new bands were sprouting up all over the city; the Clash, the Banshees, the Buzzcocks and the Damned, to name but a few. In the winter of '76, some of the biggest names in punk, including the Clash and the Pistols, united for the so-called *Anarchy Tour*. A publicity coup or nightmare, depending on the way you viewed it, the tour was dogged by scandal and allegations of lurid behaviour. Punk very quickly earned a reputation as a crass, underground movement of violent and ignorant slackers; the so-called slackers and their followers embraced this notion and could care less what the public at large, who were by now their sworn enemies, thought of them. Many were writing punk's obituary after the tour, but, against the odds, the movement continued to grow and soon working-class youths in other areas of Britain, America and beyond started to ride the wave. Punk was going viral.

In the late 70s, punk diversified and became more sophisticated. The minimalist approach was slowly replaced as bands like the Clash started to incorporate other musical influences like reggae, rockabilly and jazz into their work. Everyone remained on message, however, and punk was still a subversive, counter-cultural, rebellious and outspoken movement. Punk artists released lyrics that dealt with social problems, the oppression of the lower classes, the threat of nuclear war, the problems of unemployment and the agony of mental illness. The message was simple; not all was well and not everyone was equal, and that needed to change. If good came from the belligerent approach punk took, it was in how, through its music, it brought issues like mental illness, which, up until then, had largely been ignored and stigmatised, into the public arena for discussion.

In the 80s, a watered-down version of punk began to emerge. The anti-establishment message was replaced with a more commercially viable product; pop punk, as it came to be known. Bands like the Ramones and Generation X led the shift towards a more upbeat and fun brand of punk dealing with more light-hearted subjects like relationships. And although hardcore punk made a brief comeback, the real legacy of the eighties punk scene was to inspire a new movement termed *alternative rock*.

By the beginning of the 90s, bands like Nirvana had become superstars and were enjoying the kind of commercial success the founders of punk could only have dreamed about. Although they labelled themselves punk rockers, Nirvana were, in truth, producing a hybrid form of music, inspired by but no longer truly resembling original punk. Indeed, the very fact that this new form of music went mainstream essentially disqualifies it from being considered true punk. Nirvana's punk-rock/alternative rock/grunge style developed in tandem with the pop punk subgenre. New bands like Blink 182 and Greenday took on the mantle and carried pop punk forward into the noughties. Bands like Greenday have since enjoyed enormous commercial and critical success on the global stage. That said, rumblings of discontent continue, and many a self-styled punk would argue that, by effectively selling out to major labels and embracing the mainstream, bands like Greenday have stripped themselves of all their punk credentials. Whether you agree or not though, pop punk is here to stay and has continued to go from strength to strength in the new millennium.

Questions 8-13

Complete the flow-chart below. Write NO MORE THAN THREE WORDS for each answer.

Development of Punk Music

In 1976, the term *punk* is used for the first time to refer to a new style of music that is played at two of New York City's well-known inner-city clubs.

↓

Punk begins to find a fanbase in London as two clothes designers open up a radical new outfit store and new punk bands start to appear all **8** ....

↓

The Anarchy Tour of winter, 1976, brings together some of the biggest names in punk but the event is plagued by scandal and claims of indecent behaviour.

↓

Punk's **9** .... soon becomes tainted, but this does not stop its influence spreading beyond the punk heartlands of NYC and London.

↓

Towards the end of the decade, punk bands start to reject the **10** .... in favour of a style which embraces other types of music and fuses them with traditional punk.

↓

In the new decade, a lighter form of punk starts to **11** .... This new style is more appealing to the masses and more commercially successful. It is termed pop punk.

↓

Despite a short-lived **12** .... , traditional hardcore punk is on the wane as a musical influence and a new movement heavily influenced by punk culture is emerging - alternative rock.

↓

Alternative rock and grunge bands are, by the early 90s, a huge success, in tandem with pop punk bands. The latter remain so right into the new millenium. However, some traditional punks contend that pop punk artists, by accepting multi-million dollar contracts, have effectively sold out and have lost all their **13** ....

TASK INFORMATION: MULTIPLE CHOICE

Multiple choice tasks may test either general or detailed understanding of the text, or both. You may be asked questions which are designed to see if you have broadly understood the writer's viewpoints (or the main facts or purpose of the text), in which case you should read for gist - general understanding of the subject matter. Alternatively, you may be asked questions designed to test your grasp of specific points (or facts, pieces of information etc.) in the text, in which case you should scan the passage to locate the relevant section and then read for detail.

You must:
(i) read the questions or incomplete sentences which focus on the ideas and information contained in the text.
(ii) choose the correct option, **A**, **B**, **C** or **D**, to answer the question or complete the statement so that it corresponds with the information in the text itself.

Sample Reading Passage 2.1

In order to examine the different task types individually, this text has been broken up into sections. Read the first section now and then answer the questions which follow.

"PIGS" OF EUROPE

PIGS; that is the phrase the rest of Europe has coined for the dirty quartet that is Portugal, Ireland, Greece, Spain and Italy. This offensive and derogatory term is a sign of the times and the attitudes of the people of Europe's wealthier nations who have grown tired of hearing about Greece's debt crisis, bailout plans for Ireland and Portugal, and Spain's similarly precarious position as it teeters on the edge of the financial abyss into which the other three nations have already been sucked. The perception exists that they - the quartet - are the makers of their own undoing and doom; that their questionable fiscal policies and corrupt and inefficient governments have led them up the proverbial creek they now find themselves paddling in. People ask: 'why should WE bail them out?'; 'why should WE give away our hard-earned money in order to save THEM?'. 'Let THEM rot', they say; 'let THEM reap what they've sown'. But we should know by now, the truth is never that simple; nothing is black and white and all that exists is different shades of grey. The 'them' and 'us' attitude is quite telling — what happened to the notion of a united Europe? Most of the strongest critics of the policy of trying to save the so-called PIGS miss the fairly crucial point that if THEY go, so do WE. 'WE' are in this marriage together now, for better or for worse, and the fate of Europe rests in the ability of the PIGS to recover, otherwise, the entire monetary union will collapse and be revealed as a complete and utter shambles.

Take the case of Ireland, for example, a country whose fall from grace has been so sudden. Less than five years ago, Ireland was setting an example for small nations the world over. Think tanks were doing studies of her fiscal policy in an attempt to uncover the secrets of the Celtic Tiger. She was held up as a shining light; a perfect example of capitalism and how a nation can prosper by becoming an open economy and embracing the concept of free trade. German, French and British banks couldn't put enough money into the country — they were virtually giving it away, for goodness' sake. They lent and lent and lent to Irish banks who, much to their own discredit it has to be said, kept taking and taking and taking, like a child that doesn't know when to stop gorging itself on sweets. This reckless borrowing was unsustainable and, ultimately, all it served to do was inflate the property market to a point where collapse was a virtual certainty. At the height of

the lending euphoria, about one-eighth of all borrowing in the Eurozone went to the tiny little nation of Ireland, whose population accounts for 0.01% of the total population of the union. The idea of co-responsibility has always existed in finance. What this means is that for every reckless borrower there is a reckless lender, and, if one suffers, so, too, should the other. In other words, responsibility for Ireland's reckless borrowing lies just as much at the door of the likes of France and Germany as it does at that of Ireland itself; in order to borrow recklessly, you have to find an equally reckless lender happy to part with its funds.

In actual fact, had Ireland not been a member of the Eurozone at the time of the most recent global economic crisis sparked by the Lehman Brothers' bankruptcy, it may have been in a far better position to protect itself. Naturally, as one of the most open economies in the world, it would have been hard hit by the crisis whatever happened; however, had Ireland retained its own currency, it could have devalued immediately to make itself competitive again and regain lost ground in trade. Moreover, it could have adjusted its interest rate to account for what was happening on the ground. Instead, it was tied to a strong currency and low interest rates dictated by the European Central Bank, the combination of which only sent Ireland deeper into recession. So let's get one thing straight; being a member of the EU was not as advantageous to Ireland at the time of the economic crisis as some might automatically think. There is also the manner in which the country was forced into accepting a bailout deal. Effectively, the Irish taxpayers (like their Greek and Portuguese counterparts) have been asked to pay back the debts of every borrower who defaulted to every reckless lender who lent them money that should not have been lent in the first place. This is the first time in history when the lenders have gotten away scot-free. The only people getting a raw deal here are the ordinary tax payers of Ireland and the other PIGS.

Questions 1-8

*Choose the correct letter, **A**, **B**, **C** or **D**.*

1. Of the four countries that make up the so-called PIGS, Spain
   A is the only one which has so far avoided financial disaster.
   B is in the most precarious position.
   C is the only one that does not yet have any financial problems.
   D is the only one that has been sucked into accepting financial aid to prevent it from facing further disaster.

2. What does the writer say about the 'them and us' attitude some people have adopted?
   A In a financial crisis of this scale, every country should look after itself and not worry about what happens elsewhere.
   B It is futile to try and save the PIGS because they will cause the collapse of the entire union.
   C The members of the union are co-dependent and must support each other to have any hope of escaping the crisis.
   D The PIGS must act now to save Europe from financial disaster by supporting fellow members of the union.

3. What does the writer mean when he uses the analogy 'like a child that doesn't know when to stop gorging itself on sweets'?
   A Ireland showed no self-restraint and acted in a very immature way by continuing to engage in an activity that was sure to have very bad consequences.
   B The mentality of the Irish people is very childish and near-sighted.
   C Ireland has no control over how it behaves and relies on bigger countries to tell it what to do.
   D Irish banks should have known better than to continue lending to foreign banks as this was bound to have a bad outcome in the end.

4. Why is the statistic about the amount of Eurozone borrowing Ireland had so extraordinary?
   A Because the percentage of borrowing was so tiny compared to the country's size.
   B Because the amount of borrowing is seven-eighths less than the Eurozone average.
   C Because Ireland's borrowing is massively disproportionate to the country's size.
   D Because Ireland's borrowing level was so low compared to that of the total population of the union.

5. Who does the writer feel is responsible for Ireland's reckless borrowing policy?
   A He puts the blame on large lenders such as Germany and France for letting the situation get out of control.
   B He believes Ireland should bear most of the blame for not keeping control of its borrowing.
   C He believes that only lenders should accept co-responsibility for what happened.
   D He believes Ireland, as the borrower, is jointly responsible for the situation with those countries that lent it funds.

6. What made it difficult for Ireland to recover from the global economic crisis?
   A The European Central Bank imposed harsh rates of interest on the country's banks.
   B It made bad decisions with regard to its interest rate and currency value.
   C A combination of a strong currency, which made trading with Ireland unattractive, and low rates of interest.
   D Ireland had surrendered all control of its fiscal policy to the European Central Bank.

7. What is unique about the bailout arrangements the Portuguese, Greeks and Irish have accepted?
   A There is no arrangement in place for the lenders to take a portion of the loss.
   B Taxpayers are being asked to borrow more money to pay off their debts.
   C The people who defaulted on their loans are not being punished.
   D Only the lenders are being asked to absorb the cost of the bailout.

8. How would you sum up the writer's feelings towards the so-called PIGS and do they differ from the general consensus?
   A We can infer that the writer's views are in contrast with those of most commentators, who are much less sympathetic than him.
   B The writer adopts a similar position on the crisis to most other analysts and is quick to condemn the so-called PIGS for their reckless behaviour
   C The writer is sympathetic towards the plight of the so-called PIGS, in line with the general consensus on the issue.
   D The writer, in contrast to most analysts, feels the so-called PIGS have been wrongly blamed for creating a financial situation which was absolutely no fault of their own.

Remember:
- The questions are in the same order as the ideas in the text.
- They may refer to a small part of the text or a long section of it.
- Occasionally, one or two questions may refer to the text as a whole.
- The incorrect options may use similar words to those in the text in an effort to distract you from the correct answer, which will often be paraphrased.
- If the first task is *Multiple choice*, read through the questions quickly before reading the actual text as they will give you an idea of what the passage is about.

Method:
(i) Read each question or incomplete statement and the options A-D.
(ii) Scan the text to find the section which relates to the first question and make sure you read far enough to cover everything relevant to helping you choose the right option.
(iii) It may help to eliminate the options one-by-one starting with the obviously wrong answers and then reading the section again carefully to eliminate the rest.
(iv) Choose the ONE option you feel is correct.
(v) Repeat for the remaining questions.

TASK INFORMATION: SUMMARY COMPLETION (TYPE I)

Summary completion requires you to understand the main points of the text, or a part thereof.

You must:
(i) read the summary and identify the part(s) of the text to which it is related.
(ii) complete the gaps in the summary by choosing a word or words from the text.

Sample Reading Passage 2.2

In order to examine the different task types individually, this text has been broken up into sections. Read the second section now and then answer the questions which follow.

PIGS OF EUROPE cont.

So, what would actually happen if Ireland were to go default? History tells us that there would be a period of extreme economic difficulty and hyper-inflation of between 2 and 5 years. The economy would thereafter recover and the country would return to relative prosperity as was the case with the Argentinian default of the late nineties and early noughties.

And if Ireland did default, where would that leave the rest of Europe? Ironically, because of their reckless lending, the big three, Germany, France and the U.K. would be hugely exposed and would face losses of quite astronomical proportions. They could conceivably be left in an even worse position than Ireland. The Eurozone project would collapse and the single currency would die with it.

When we consider the facts, then, it is quite clear that it is not by any means Europe's generosity that is funding the PIGS in their efforts to stay afloat, but rather Europe's survival and self-preservation instincts kicking in. Basically, it is in the rest of Europe's interest as much, and arguably more, than it is the PIGS'

that a way is found out of the present predicament. And so to all those calling for the PIGS to be thrown out or punished for bringing shame on the Euro, let it be known that the shame of a reckless lender is no less great than that of the borrower. The child can only gorge itself on sweets if the parent continues to supply them, and what kind of parent would do such a stupid thing?

Questions 9-13

Complete the summary below.

Choose ONE WORD ONLY from the passage for each answer.

The consequences of an Irish Default

A period of severe **9** .... turbulence with rising living costs is likely to follow any potential default. This period could last anywhere between two and five years based on the example of the Argentinian default which happened in the late 1990s. Having endured this period of adjustment, the country is then likely to enjoy a more pleasant time of **10** ....

Contrary to popular belief, however, an Irish default might not leave Ireland in such a bad position. In actual fact, some of its prime lenders may be faced with an even more serious predicament; such is their level of exposure to potential loss. If the worst were to happen, it would spell the end of the **11** .... and, equally, the single currency experiment would have utterly failed.

In view of this information, the eagerness of the large European countries to assist the so-called PIGS financially should not necessarily be viewed as a form of extreme generosity, but as a way of preserving their own financial systems and ensuring that **12** .... as a whole survives this crisis. In truth, the sense of **13** .... and guilt felt by the Portuguese, Irish, Greeks and Spaniards, should be shared by the other European nations who lent them money so recklessly and who were, therefore, totally complicit in causing the terrible crisis that ensued.

Remember:

- The information you need may be in one paragraph/part of the text or spread over a longer part.
- If the first task is the summary task, read over it before you begin reading the actual passage because it will provide you with an excellent overview of the subject matter.
- Underline the important words in the summary before you start; finding where these words are located in the text will help you to identify the section to which the summary relates.
- Write each word(s) you use to fill in the gaps exactly as it appears in the passage; do not change the form of the word(s) in any way. If you must change the form of the word(s) for it to fit the sentence, you have not chosen the correct word(s).

Method:

(i) Read the instructions and check how many words you have to write.

(ii) Locate the part(s) of the text you need by reading the summary (pay close attention to the title and key words.)

(iii) Look at each numbered gap and decide what kind of word(s) you need to find to fill it.

(iv) Read the relevant part of the original text and highlight the word(s) you think fits each gap.

(v) Write the words in the gaps and then re-read the summary to check that it **(a)** makes sense and **(b)** accurately summarises what is said in the original text.

TASK INFORMATION: SUMMARY COMPLETION (TYPE 2)

Summary completion requires you to understand the main points of the text, or a part thereof.
You must:

(i) read the summary and identify the part(s) of the text to which it is related.

(ii) write the correct letter in the numbered gaps of the summary by choosing an answer from the options given in the box below.

Sample Reading Passage 3.1

In order to examine the different task types individually, this text has been broken up into sections. Read the first section now and then answer the questions which follow.

THE ROMA PEOPLE A *Legacy of Injustice*

Who are the Roma? They are depicted by the media as a nomadic tribe of people who travel, by choice, from place to place and appear seemingly unable or unwilling to integrate into modern society. In literature, the Roma lifestyle has been romanticised and demonised in equal measure, and they (the Roma people) have been often cast with an air of mysticism, or, conversely, as having a penchant for the dark arts, depending on the writer's agenda. Of course, the truth is far removed from both the negative perception created by the media of a people stuck in the past and the two opposing images created by the literary world. And we will get to the truth in detail later, but first, I suppose, it's probably worth acknowledging that, until very recently at least, most of our wealthy European brethren; the French, Germans, Italians and so on, would have answered my initial question with the same rather nonplussed retort as we British might: 'who cares?'. And it would have been a fair comment; the Roma, most of them anyway, were just far enough away, shut behind the closed borders of Eastern Europe, that we really didn't have to worry about them one way or the other. Out of sight, of course, means out of mind.

Questions 1-5

*Complete the summary using the list of words, **A-L**, below.*

Misconceptions

The Roma are a people misunderstood. The media **1** .... them as a tribe of traveller people who **2** .... embrace the nomadic lifestyle with which they have become synonymous. The Roma of the media are not prepared to **3** .... the ways of the modern world.

The world of literature is hardly much kinder to them. In prose, either they are portrayed as almost supernatural beings with mystical qualities, or they are labelled as having an uncommon **4** .... for black magic.

Neither of these representations is **5** .... of the truth, but perhaps we know so little about them and have not cared to know more, until now at least, because the Roma people have not been living in our midst.

(a) grudgingly   (b) displays   (c) willingly   (d) reflective   (e) sheepishly   (f) renounce

(g) fondness   (h) accept   (i) distaste   (j) objective   (k) paints   (l) dismissive

Remember:
- The summary may relate to part(s) or all of the text.
- Options which fit the gaps in the summary grammatically and make sense may not necessarily be correct in meaning; the summary must reflect what is said in the original text.
- There will always be several options which you do not need.

Method:
(i)   Read the summary and take note of all the options which potentially fit each gap.

(ii) Locate and read the part(s) of the text you need, using key words from the summary to guide you.

(iii) Choose an option for each gap, ensuring that the chosen word gives the summary the same meaning as the original text.

(iv) Re-read the summary and ensure you are satisfied that it is an accurate reflection of the information in the text.

TASK INFORMATION: SHORT-ANSWER QUESTIONS

Short-answer question tasks test detailed understanding of the text. You will be asked questions designed to test your grasp of specific points (or facts, pieces of information etc.) in the text, in which case you should scan the passage to locate the relevant section and then read for detail.

You must:
i) read the questions.
ii) find a suitable answer in the text that is within the word limit specified in the task instructions.

Sample Reading Passage 3.2

In order to examine the different task types individually, this text has been broken up into sections. Read the second section now and then answer the questions which follow.

THE ROMA PEOPLE *Legacy of Injustice* cont.

But all that changed recently with the accession of several Eastern bloc countries into the European Union; the vast landscape of continental Europe was now open for business to the Roma people, many of whom migrated to wealthier countries, like France and Italy, in search of things we all look for; better treatment, better opportunities and, above all, a better life. Europe now had no choice but to care.

It is often said that society is judged by how it treats the weakest, and perhaps meekest, in its midst. Do we exploit the vulnerable, help them, or pretend they don't exist and brush the problem under the carpet — or, worse still, brush it into another room for someone else to deal with? In the case of the Roma, the evidence so far points to European Union member states doing, rather alarmingly, the last of these. Both France and Italy have been immersed in controversy now for some time over their handling of Roma immigrants. In Italy, Roma camps have been forcibly removed from large cities such as Naples — a course of action that even has the governmental seal of approval. The Roma, you see, have been labelled a public health and security risk. In France, they have fared little better. In the summer of 2010, the state sanctioned the deportation of about 1,000 Roma and destroyed 539 Roma camps around the country. The government, of course, maintained that the deportation initiative did not specifically target the Roma people, but any and all foreign gangs and communities involved in crime. Unfortunately for the French authorities, a leaked memo that August revealed that Roma camps were being specifically targeted: Therefore, this was not an issue of crime and immigration; it had become one of ethnicity. This revelation had the E.U. and U.N. publicly criticizing French policy, while human rights organizations such as Amnesty International were, understandably, up in arms.

Questions 6-8
Write NO MORE THAN THREE WORDS for each answer.

6. What has the way the French and Italian governments have dealt with the Roma people caused a lot of?

_____

7. What did the French authorities dismantle many of in the summer of 2010?

_____

8. What came in for criticism following the revelations found in a leaked official memo?

_____

> **Remember:**
> - Your answers must be taken directly from the text and you must copy the words you use in your answers exactly as they appear in the text.
> - Do not exceed the word limit specified in the instructions.
> - The questions will follow the order the answers appear in the text.

> **Method:**
> **(i)** Read the first question and underline the key words in it.
> **(ii)** Find the part of the text to which the question relates.
> **(iii)** Select the word(s) in the text which answer the question correctly.
> **(iv)** Repeat for subsequent questions.

TASK INFORMATION: YES/NO/NOT GIVEN

YES / NO / NOT GIVEN tasks require you to identify and understand the ideas, views and attitudes expressed in the text.
You must:

(i) read statements which focus on the writer's ideas as expressed in the text.

(ii) scan the text to find where the writer discusses the information contained in the statements.

(iii) decide if the idea presented in each statement agrees with the opinions/ideas of the writer (**Yes**), contradicts them (**No**), or if there is no information about the idea in the text (**Not given**).

Sample Reading Passage 3.3

In order to examine the different task types individually, this text has been broken up into sections. Read the third section now and then answer the questions which follow.

THE ROMA PEOPLE *Legacy of Injustice* cont.

As things stand now, the controversy has died down, though the issue has not gone away. But rather than condemn the French and Italians, which would be all too easy, let us instead concede that dealing with migrant communities can be difficult. Perhaps though, before Europe makes any more policy decisions in this regard, we should get to know the Roma a little better first, and appreciate their distinct and very rich cultural identity. Then, at least, we will be better informed.

The Roma people are undoubtedly one of the groups that has, over the years, fallen victim to the most serious consequences of racism. A closer look reveals that they are not ethnically or culturally driven to lead a nomadic lifestyle, but have done so thanks largely to the complex developments of history. And it is these same developments that have trapped many Roma people in poverty today through no fault of their own.

Historical evidence places the Roma in Eastern Europe from around the 4th Century B.C., and it is thought that they originated in Northern India. From the 14th to 19th Century, many of the Roma were enslaved by the empires which controlled Eastern Europe. Those lucky enough to be free commonly contributed to society as smiths, musicians and soldiers, according to historical records. But even these people feared enslavement, and it is this fear that led many amongst them to change location so often. This created the perception of a nomadic lifestyle that persists today. While the enslavement of the Roma might have ended in the 19th century, another critical juncture came during World War Two, when the Nazis killed an estimated one and a half million. These devastating events continue to play a significant role in the Roma psyche, and, even today, nearly 70 years on from the Nazi genocide, many Roma fear officially revealing their identity. Most of the estimated 7-12 million in Eastern Europe now live in relative poverty; the unemployment rate for Roma people is a staggering 40% and fewer than one fifth have even received primary-level education. Their backs are against the wall and they need our help. History has certainly dealt the Roma a worse hand than most, and society definitely owes them something more than its disdain. There was a time, not so long ago, when, finally free from slavery in the 19th century, the Roma earned a reputation for being hard-working and skilled tradespeople. The challenges they have faced since, not least the extermination of around one sixth of their people, have made it difficult for them to keep pace with the speed of industrialisation and learn the skills necessary to prosper in today's world. But surely, after all they have been through as a people, they deserve our sympathy and our help, not to mention our respect. Isn't it about time that we lent a hand to these unfortunate folk?

Questions 9-14

Do the following statements agree with the views of the writer in Sample Reading Passage 3.3?

In boxes 9-14 on your answer sheet, write

		T	F	NG
YES	*if the statement agrees with the views of the writer*			
NO	*if the statement contradicts the views of the writer*			
NOT GIVEN	*if there is no information on this*			

9   The French and Italian governments are deserving of the severest criticism for their actions. ☐ ☐ ☐

10 The Roma people have a rich and unique heritage. ☐ ☐ ☐

11 The Roma people have always been inclined towards a nomadic existence. ☐ ☐ ☐

12 The Roma were complicit in creating the situation of poverty they find themselves in. ☐ ☐ ☐

13 The Roma people have faced more than their fair share of misfortune down through the ages. ☐ ☐ ☐

14 The Roma people are only now starting to catch up with the rest of the world skills-wise. ☐ ☐ ☐

Remember:

• Check whose views you are being asked to verify. In this case (and normally), it is the writer's; therefore, any other person's viewpoint that might be mentioned in the text is irrelevant.

• There will always be at least one YES, one NO and one NOT GIVEN answer.

Method:

(i)   Look at the statements and underline the important words therein.

(ii)   Find the part of the text which discusses the ideas in the first statement and read it carefully for detail.

(iii)   Decide whether the statement agrees with the writer's views or not (or isn't broached at all).

(iv)   Repeat for the other statements.

TASK INFORMATION: MATCHING HEADINGS

This task requires you to have a general understanding of the information contained in the text at paragraph level.

You must:
(i) read the headings and match them to some or all of the paragraphs in the original text.

Sample Reading Passage 4

SIEGE OF SARAJEVO

A

In medieval times, the practice of besieging a town or city for perhaps years on end in order to starve and/or terrorise it into submission was quite commonplace, and this period was known as the Dark Ages with good reason because, along with sieges, there was a general sense of disorganisation verging on anarchy, and an intellectual and moral vacuum in which corruption, skulduggery, deceit, violence and brutality could prosper. It is hardly a surprise then that as time moved on and humanity progressed to a more dignified and civilised state of existence, there were fewer and fewer instances of cities being besieged, and any sieges there were generally ended fairly promptly, so the victims were spared, for want of a better world, from having to endure prolonged hardship. By the latter half of the 20th century, the practice had virtually disappeared. Ravaged by two brutal world wars, Europe, as it began to rise from the ashes, started to realise that strength came from unity not discord, and that in the fever of war, unspeakable acts can be committed; acts that should be avoided at all costs forever more.

B

After World War Two then, Europe and the rest of the world bought into the idea of creating a protectorate responsible for upholding justice and defending the weak. Tyranny would no longer be tolerated and crimes against humanity (a new phrase coined to describe crimes directed at large groups of people of the same race/country/ethnicity or who are connected to one another in some other way which lends them a common identity) would be punishable with a sentence which would reflect the severity of the crime. We know this protectorate today as the United Nations. Alongside it, other international coalitions were emerging. NATO, for example, is a group of countries sworn to protect one another and the weak from aggression. In such an atmosphere, one would imagine a return to the siege mentality of the dark ages as, well, unimaginable; or, at least, one would expect an aggressor besieging a city to be reprimanded in the harshest terms and the city to be promptly emancipated. After all, this was a new era of enlightenment and peace.

C

How then can the Siege of Sarajevo be explained away? Yugoslavia, an amalgam of peoples of different ethnicities, kept together by the glue of Marshal Tito's leadership until his death in 1980, was always a potential zone of conflict. There had been sporadic outbreaks of violence and rumblings of rebellion by the different factions for years. Sooner or later, all hell would break loose - unless the situation was contained; unless the international community, or more specifically the U.N., self-proclaimed guardian of the free world, was to calm the situation. Instead, the world stood by and watched as, on the 2nd of March, 1992, war broke out in the Balkans. The rights and wrongs of the war do not fall within the scope of this discussion, which is only concerned with examining the international community's failure to intervene, but it is necessary to look at the facts surrounding the siege. Paramilitaries barricaded sniper positions near Sarajevo's parliament, but their initial efforts at insurgency were thwarted by people power as thousands of citizens took to the streets in protest. A day later, Bosnia and Herzegovina declared its independence from Yugoslavia and more sporadic fighting broke out. On the 5th of April, peace marchers of all the Yugoslav ethnicities - Serb, Croat and Muslim - marched in unity for peace. Sadly, no one was listening to them and two young women in the crowd were shot by unidentified gunman - the alarm bells in Europe should have been ringing.

D

A day later, Europe and America officially recognised the new Bosnian state. The fledgling Bosnian government expected peace troops to be deployed to assist it and to quell the violence before it got totally out of hand, but Europe was slow to react. The Yugoslav People's Army attacked the city of Sarajevo that same day – Bosnia's capital was under siege and its army was ill-equipped to defend its people. Bosniak homes were ransacked; civilians were rounded up; men and women were separated and many of both sexes were taken away to detention camps. On May the 2nd, the Yugoslav People's Army forces established a total blockade of the city, and this is when the siege began in earnest. Civilians were denied road access, food and medical supplies were cut off and the city's utilities (water, electricity, heating etc.) were sabotaged. For much of the next six months, the city was bombarded with shells on an almost-daily basis. Trapped residents lived in a state of permanent fear. Paramilitaries had a virtual free-hand and were allowed to run amok. In June of 1993, the attacks became particularly intense again. On the 1st day of the month, 15 died and 80 people were injured in an assault on an association football event in the city. The onslaught was relentless and on the 5th of February the following year, 68 civilians were killed and another 200 injured in what became known as the Markale Marketplace Massacre.

E

It was in response to this last incident, nearly two years after the outbreak of war, that the U.N. finally stepped in militarily. Eventually, in October 1995, a ceasefire was reached and the Siege of Sarajevo was officially declared at an end following the withdrawal of the last-remaining Federal troops from the hills around the city on February 29th, 1996. It had been nearly four years since the siege had first begun; much of the city had been reduced to rubble, thousands of innocent civilians had died, and for what? There are many theories as to why it might have taken the international community so long to react, but theory-smeary; we may never get an answer, and, if we don't, then at least let us hope the lessons of Sarajevo have been learned and there will be no next time.

Questions 1-5

*Reading Passage 4 has five paragraphs, **A-E**.*
*Choose the correct heading for **A-E** from the list of headings below.*

*Write the correct number, **i-vii**, in boxes 1-5 on your answer sheet.*

List of Headings

(i) A shift in mentality
(ii) Warning signs ignored
(iii) Marching for Peace
(iv) 20th century Sieges
(v) A decisive move by the international community
(vi) Too little, too late
(vii) An institution for peace
(viii) Sustained attack

1   Paragraph **A**   _____

2   Paragraph **B**   _____

3   Paragraph **C**   _____

4   Paragraph **D**   _____

5   Paragraph **E**   _____

Remember:

● This question is testing your general rather than detailed understanding of the text.
● The headings are about the main ideas in the paragraphs, not about one or two details.
● If you are not sure about the answer for one paragraph, come back to it at the end when you have eliminated most of the options.
● Always read the headings before you read the text to get an idea of what you should look out for.

Method:

(i)   Check how many headings there are and how many paragraphs there are to label.
(ii) Read the first paragraph of the text for gist (quickly for general understanding).
(iii) Underline the main ideas and choose the most suitable heading.
(iv) Do the same for the other paragraphs, ensuring you only select each heading once.

TASK INFORMATION: MATCHING SENTENCE ENDINGS

This task requires you to understand a number of significant ideas or key points in the text.
You must:
- (i) read the first halves of some sentences. These are in the same order as the information will appear in the text.
- (ii) choose the ending for each half-sentence from a number of options so that the complete sentence accurately expresses an idea / opinion / fact in the text.

Questions 6-10

*Complete each sentence with the correct ending, **A-H**, below.*

6. In order to heal the scars of war, in the second half of the 20th century Europe _____
7. This desire for peace, justice and stability prompted the nations of the world to invest _____
8. In the case of Sarajevo, however, the protests and concerns of people on the ground were being _____
9. A relentless bombardment of the city culminated in _____
10. This tragedy, which took place two full years into the conflict, finally _____

A	compelled the United Nations to sanction the use of force and intervene in the dispute.
B	forced the two opposing factions to negotiate a peace under the supervision of the U.N..
C	looked to operate a united front going forward to minimise the potential for further dispute.
D	the infamous Marketplace Massacre which claimed 68 innocent victims.
E	the capitulation of the Bosnian forces and the ending of the siege.
F	heavily in their military capabilities in order to create a deterrent against future conflict.
G	in the establishment of a new international body designed to protect the vulnerable from oppression.
H	ignored when Europe should have instead recognised the escalating threat of serious conflict.

Remember:
- There will always be two or three extra options that are there to distract you.
- Ensure that the option you match makes sense grammatically.
- The first halves of the sentences contain clues to help you locate the parts of the original text you need - look out for key words.
- Incorrect options may make sense but this does not mean that they have the same meaning as the information in the original text - always refer back to the original text to check for meaning.
- The questions will appear in the same order as the information in the text - even the sentence halves; that is, the information contained within each sentence half will be found before that of the ending it should be matched with.

Method:
- (i) Read the first incomplete sentence, highlighting any key words you find.
- (ii) Identify the part(s) you need by scanning the text, and ensure that you read the relevant section(s) carefully.
- (iii) Read the options carefully and select the one you think is the most accurate reflection of what is written in the text.
- v) Repeat for the other questions.

REVISION: SHORT-ANSWER QUESTIONS

Questions 11-13

Write NO MORE THAN TWO WORDS for each answer.

11. What were the protestors calling for when they marched on the 5th of April?

_____

12. What did Federal forces set up in May 1992?

_____

13. What preceded the declaration of an end to hostilities in 1996, but created the environment in which negotiations could commence?

_____

TASK INFORMATION: MATCHING NAMES

This task requires you to relate information, ideas or opinions in the text to a number of people, places, events etc..

You must:

(i) read the list of statements and match them to a list of options by finding the information in the text.

(ii) write the letter of the statement which matches the question in the answer box (note: the letter of the statement, not the letter of the paragraph).

Sample Reading Passage 5

YOU'RE FIRED!

A

The U.K. version of the American T.V. show The Apprentice is now in its seventh series and is proving just as big a hit on this side of the pond as it did when first shown in the States. The BBC has really hit on a winning formula it seems, with the grisly countenance and pull-no-punches approach of Lord Alan Sugar striking a chord with viewers. *Entertainment Magazine* writer Josh Umbridge says of the show's star man; 'Sugar's execution is brilliant. His hard work has brought him all the trappings of wealth, but he is still as unpretentious, grounded and, dare I say it, vulgar as ever. That's what we love about him!'

B

But not everyone is a fan of Lord Sugar. Psychologist and feminist Rachel Deevers complains: 'Sugar is a misogynistic relic of the past. We should not be glorifying these characters as doing so endorses their policies and behaviour. It wasn't so long ago that Sugar would demand to know of potential female candidates at job interviews whether they planned to have children in the near future - this being a determining factor in hiring decisions apparently. Yet now we hold him up as some sort of example to follow — almost a role model. I don't agree.'

C

Business analyst Paula Schriver, who has worked with Sugar on numerous projects in the past, takes issue with Deevers' portrayal though: 'This is, in effect, character assassination. Those accusations are purely hearsay. The facts speak for themselves; some of Lord Sugar's most trusted employees and confidants have been and remain women. Lord Sugar is not a sexist — what a ridiculous assertion to make. The truth is, Alan does not mince his words and this has made him a good many enemies over time. These kinds of rumours are just a way people have of trying to get back at Alan and tarnish his reputation, but they won't work. Alan is a man of integrity and his record speaks for itself.'

D

Former employee Elena Fernandes agrees that Sugar has never had a problem with women, though she does question his management style: 'Sugar is what I would class a very old-style autocratic manager. The amount of respect he gives a work colleague is dependent on their position in his hierarchy. And he can be quite the bully sometimes. A lot of his methods would be frowned upon by experts in human resources and people management. When he wants to get his way, there is no stopping him — he is quite a formidable opponent in every sense — and to make matters worse, his motivational style is simply the do-it-or-else approach — hardly inspirational.'

E

Schriver, though, is quick to come to his defence, pointing out that everything about Lord Sugar — from the story of his early years and the struggle for success to his subsequent achievements — is an inspiration. 'Alan came from nothing; his family was not rich. He lived in a working class area of London and had to start on the very bottom rung of the ladder. In this context, to dismiss his achievements and simply label him an uninspiring person is grossly unfair. Alan represents hope and, more importantly, proof for young working class men and women that there is light at the end of the tunnel and that they can make something of themselves.'

F

To his critics, Lord Sugar himself provides a rather stoical response: 'if I were in the business of pleasing everyone, I would not have lasted very long in that other important business — of making money. If it's a choice, therefore, between pleasing a few people so as to keep on their good side and rubbing them up the wrong way to create a viable business project, then the decision is obvious. I didn't get along in this business by making friends but by making tough decisions.' His harshest critic, Deevers, acknowledges that to make oneself successful in business requires a degree of toughness and single-mindedness: 'Sugar has these traits in abundance. My issue is with his general attitude towards women and with the kinds of controversial and damning remarks he comes out with all the time. I am all for telling it like it is, but when I watch Sugar I cringe because what he does is cruel. His criticism is relentless and he makes people feel very small indeed.'

G

The debate over the rights and wrongs of Sugar's behaviour will surely go on and on, but one thing's for sure; the man himself will be paying little attention. He will be too busy selecting who's going to be his next apprentice — and we'll be too busy tuning in to find out to care.

Questions 1-4

Look at the following people (questions 1-4) and the list of statements below.
*Match each person with the correct statement, **A-G**. Write the correct letter, **A-G**, in boxes 1-4 on your answer sheet.*

1. Paula Schriver _____

2. Lord Sugar _____

3. Elena Fernandes _____

4. Rachel Deevers _____

A Sugar's approach to management is highly unconventional.

B People who cast aspersions on Lord Sugar's character are motivated by a desire to ruin his good name.

C Lord Sugar's record on ensuring equality in the workplace is very questionable.

D There is no point in ever trying to please people because business comes first.

E Lord Sugar only respects those higher up in the hierarchy than him.

F The best interests of the business should be put before personal feelings.

G Sugar's management style motivates employees to take the initiative.

Remember:
- Sometimes the names will be referred to in more than one place in the text.
- There will always be a number of statements you do not need.
- Write the letter of the correct statement, not of the paragraph where you find the answer.
- Each name can be matched with only one statement.

Method:
(i) Look at the list of names; underline them wherever they appear in the original text.
(ii) For each name, read everything that the person says.
iii) Choose the statement which accurately reflects one of the things they say.

TASK INFORMATION: SENTENCE COMPLETION

This task requires you to understand key points in the original text. You must:

   (i) read the first sentence and highlight the key words/concepts.
   (ii) scan the original text to locate where the relevant information appears.
   (iii) select the appropriate word(s) from the text and write them in the space provided.
   (iv) repeat for the remainder of the questions.

Questions 5-13

Write NO MORE THAN TWO WORDS for each answer.

5. Lord Sugar's straight-talking style is very appealing to _____ of the T.V. show in which he features.

6. He is, however, accused of having let his _____ be swayed by information which he has no place asking for in interviews to begin with.

7. In his defence, however, such is the number of _____ he has made down through the years that Sugar could possibly be the victim of a campaign to blacken his good name.

8. Sugar's style of management has been referred to as _____ in that he makes all important decisions himself.

9. His ideas on how to manage people go against what most _____ would recommend.

10. Sugar's story is an inspiration for _____ people all over Britain.

11. Sugar maintains that sacrificing a personal relationship with someone is justified if it is in the interests of the _____ being undertaken.

12. Even Sugar's harshest critics cede that he has plenty of _____ , a quality that, along with single-minded focus, will take you far in business.

13. In truth, Sugar is likely to pay little notice to how popular he is; he is more interested in securing the right candidate as his _____ .

Remember:

- Do not exceed the maximum amount of words allowed in each gap.
- Think about the type of word(s) which can fill each gap i.e. a noun / verb etc.
- Do not change the words you use in any way; they should be copied exactly as they appear in the text. If you think you have to change a word, then you have not chosen the correct one.
- The sentences will be in the same order as the information appears in the text.

Method:

   (i) Read the first incomplete sentence, highlighting any key words you find.
   (ii) identify the part(s) you need by scanning the text, and ensure that you read the relevant section(s) carefully.
   (iii) Select the appropriate word(s) to fill the gap in the sentence and ensure that the meaning of the sentence accurately reflects what is said in the text.
   (iv) Repeat for the other questions.

REMEMBER: Note, Table, Sentence, Summary (Type 1) and Flow-chart completion exercises are very similar. We have already looked at Flow-chart, Summary and Sentence completion. Now we will look at **Note** and **Table** completion.

Sample Reading Passage 6

A LOOK AT DUBLIN ZOO

Overview:

Dublin Zoo is situated in the Phoenix Park, not only Ireland's but Europe's largest urban park area. But the abundance of space is only one of many things which weigh in in its favour and make it such an appealing tourist attraction for visitors to the country. Another is its charitable status; the zoo is a not-for-profit organisation dedicated to animal welfare and conservation. It is also at once one of the world's oldest and most modern zoos, and the 28-hectare park is home to over 100 species of animals, not to mention gardens, lakes and wonderful natural habitats.

Opened in 1831, it has, needless to say, undergone quite the transformation between then and now. And it is this remarkable transformation that has made it Ireland's leading tourist attraction for foreign visitors, drawing in over one million annually.

One of the zoos primary goals is to educate visitors; the other is conservation. The two, in fact, go hand-in-hand. Key to the successful conservation of rare and endangered species is habitat preservation, but until people understand the fundamental relationship between habitat and species, the preparedness to put ourselves out a little in order to protect precious habitats will not exist.

Of course, the zoo is also totally committed to the welfare of its animal residents. Each year, it strives to improve its artificial habitats; making them a more realistic and natural experience for the animals and a more exciting, educational and interactive one for visitors.

New Attractions:

The African Savannah has been under development for many years and it is now beginning to take shape and become something very special indeed. The sense that you are walking through the grassy savannah and the open African plains is very real indeed. Highlights include the giraffe and zebra enclosure, and the hunting dog grounds. Not to be missed either are the rhino, oryx and ostrich areas. The chimpanzee zone is also a big draw for tourists as the daily feedings involve a search for honey and special treats; seeing these animals use their intelligence to overcome the little challenges the zookeepers set them is quite delightful.

The Gorilla Rainforest was completed in the summer of 2011, just in time for the peak tourist season. In this enclosure, visitors are taken on a journey to the tropics; it is a spacious and naturalistic habitat with dense vegetation imitating the sense of lush undergrowth found in rainforests. Pathways guide visitors though the forest and along the swamp boardwalk as they watch the gorillas at rest and at play from specially-designed observation points.

The Asian rainforest is another highlight of a trip to Dublin Zoo. Home to one of the few breeding elephant groups in captivity, this habitat boasts pools, dramatic rock formations and a waterfall, all of which are encircled by a dense forest of trees and bamboo. The Kaziranga Forest Trail, as it is better known, has been tailor-made for these unique creatures, and this may explain the zoo's unusually productive breeding programme. Its ever-expanding family of Asian

elephants includes matriarch Bernhardine, born in 1984, her daughter Asha, born in May 2007, as well as Bernhardine's sister and her daughter and son, both 'children' of the new millennium.

Revival:

As recently as 1990, Dublin Zoo was almost forced to close. Lacking enough funding to cover its day-to-day costs, it took the intervention of the state to rescue it. Dublin Zoo now receives an annual grant from the government, in line with the policy most European countries have adopted towards zoological gardens and safari parks. What sets Dublin Zoo apart from the majority of its counterparts, however, is that this lifeline did not just serve to sustain the park, but rather gave it the impetus to recover and expand.

In 1997, the President of Ireland donated 17 hectares of the grounds of her official residence to the zoo. This also made a huge difference by enabling keepers to create new habitats and expand existing ones in order to make the zoo a much more pleasant environment for its animal inhabitants. Indeed, today, it is more akin to a safari park in many respects, so spacious are the large-animal enclosures.

Secret of Success

Dublin Zoo has transformed itself into one of the most successful zoos in the world by being ambitious, but at the same time remaining true to its core values and putting the animals first, while placing visitor-experience a close second. The park is extremely well planned out and the environment is a very pleasant one indeed. Visitors are left satisfied for two reasons; (1) they get value for money and (2) they leave feeling good about themselves for supporting an organisation that clearly looks after the best interests of the animals in its care. Families and those with young children appreciate the lengths the zoo has gone to to make the park 'little-visitor' friendly more than most; such has been the consideration that has gone into designing child-oriented features.

Conclusions:

Any zoo struggling to attract visitors should take a leaf out of Dublin Zoo's book. It was not content to claim a subsidy from the state in order to sustain it. Instead, it used the government's financial aid as a stepping stone to help it develop into an organisation that is largely self-sustaining. Its mantra has been to always strive to move forward and improve, and, in fulfilling this mantra, the public, recognising value for money when they see it, have endorsed Dublin Zoo like never before.

TASK INFORMATION: NOTE COMPLETION

This task requires you to understand key ideas, information, opinions or facts expressed in the original text. You must:
  (i) read through the notes, highlighting key words.
  (ii) scan the text to locate the section(s) containing the information related to each gap.
  (iii) select the word or words from the original text which complete each gap and write them in the appropriate space on the answer sheet.

Questions 1-10
Complete the notes below. Write NO MORE THAN TWO WORDS for each answer.

Notes on Dublin Zoo for tomorrow's briefing:

Overview
● contained within largest **1** _____ of any European city
● charitable organisation committed to conservation projects and animal welfare
● covers an area of 28 hectares and houses over 100 species of animals
● attracts more than one million **2** _____ every year
● one of Europe's oldest yet most modern zoos
● primary objectives are (i) to educate visitors (ii) conservation

New attractions
The **3** _____ of the Chimpanzees attract many visitors to the African Savannah zone. The Gorilla Rainforest has only recently been **4** _____, so it is not possible to comment on its appeal yet. The Kaziranga Forest Trail boasts a family of elephants that are the product of a very successful **5** _____.

Revival
● saved from closure in 1990 by a government **6** _____ renewed annually
● once the financial situation of the zoo was secure, park management were determined to push forward with plans to **7** _____ the park
● president gave 17 hectares of land from her official place of residence to the park in 1997
● land used to develop new **8** _____ and improve the ones that were already there

Success and conclusions
● the zoo's ambition has driven it on to greater successes without it ever losing sight of its **9** _____
● the welfare of the animals is the zoo's top priority, followed closely by the visitors' experience
● there is a high level of customer satisfaction for two reasons: **(i)** the zoo offers value for money **(ii)** customers feel like they are **10** _____ a good cause
● Dublin Zoo's success stems from its desire to continually develop and improve in every key aspect of its operation

---

Remember:
● The notes will roughly follow the order in which the information appears in the text.
● Use exact words copied from the text to fill the gaps.
● Adhere to the word limit for each gap.
● The notes may be paraphrased so look for key words and key concepts to help you find the information in the original text.
● A the notes are in order, use already-completed sections to help you pinpoint where to look for missing information in the original text.

Method:
(i) If the note completion exercise is the first task, read it before reading the original text as it will give you a good overview of the subject matter.
(ii) Highlight the key words or concepts around the first gap.
(iii) Identify the part(s) of the text you need by scanning, and ensure that you read the relevant section(s) carefully.
(iii) Select the appropriate word(s) to fill the gap and ensure that the meaning accurately reflects what is said in the text.
(iv) Repeat for the other questions.

TASK INFORMATION: MULTIPLE CHOICE (TYPE 2)

This task only differs from the first type of multiple choice question we looked at in that you are required to select more than one correct answer.

Questions 11 and 12
*Choose **TWO** letters, **A-E**.*

Which **two** of the following statements best describe the Gorilla Rainforest?
- **A**   a tropical habitat sparsely populated with trees and other vegetation
- **B**   an area of natural pathways which offer a good vantage point for viewing the gorillas
- **C**   an authentic-looking habitat that mimics the look of a real rainforest floor
- **D**   an area boasting walking routes which offer some excellent opportunities to observe the gorillas
- **E**   a swampy area of land on which the gorillas are known to frequently rest and play

Questions 13 and 14
*Choose TWO letters, **A-E**.*

What conclusions does the writer draw about Dublin Zoo's success?
- **A**   it is largely down to the aid package it receives annually from the government
- **B**   it is largely down to its insistence on being self-sufficient and refusing the government subsidy
- **C**   it is in part thanks to the zoo's determination to progress and improve
- **D**   it no longer needs the government's financial aid package
- **E**   it is in part thanks to the zoo giving customers an experience they value and pursuing a policy they support

> **Remember:**
> - Always check the instructions to see how many options you should select.
> - The questions will be in the order they appear in the text, though the answer-options (A-E) might not be.

TASK INFORMATION: TABLE COMPLETION

This task requires you to understand and categorise key information outlined in the original text.
You must:
- (i) scan the text to find specific information using the headings and words in the table to help you.
- (ii) find one, two or three words or a number in the text which answer each question and copy them into the gaps.

> **Remember:**
> - The information will not necessarily be in the same order in the text as it is presented in the table.
> - Use exact words copied from the text to fill the gaps.
> - Adhere to the word limit for each gap.
> - Always read the headings for each row and column and underline key words which will help you locate the information you need.

> **Method:**
> - **(i)** Look at the instructions and check how many words you must write.
> - **(ii)** Read the column and row headings; this will help you find the part(s) of the text you need.
> - **(iii)** Read the table, underline the key words and decide what kinds of words are needed to fill the gaps (i.e. nouns, verbs etc.)
> - **(iv)** Find the part(s) of the text you need and read it carefully.
> - **(v)** Underline the words in the text which fill the gaps and copy them in.
> - **(vi)** Read the information in the table again to ensure that it makes sense and does not contradict what is said in the original text.

Sample Reading Passage 7

HURRICANES

A

Intense or violent depressions are known to most of us as hurricanes, though they have different names depending on the area over which they form. In the Atlantic and Eastern Pacific, the familiar term is used; however, in the Western Pacific, these weather systems are more commonly referred to as typhoons, and in the Indian Ocean they are given yet another name – cyclones. But by whatever name they are known, all hurricanes essentially begin life the same way; as strong clusters of thunderstorms. These thunderstorms sometimes make their way out to sea, and when they drift over warm ocean waters they can start to pick up intensity at a remarkable rate.

B

The warm air from the storm cluster combines with the warm air at the ocean's surface and starts to rise. This creates low pressure at the surface. Trade winds blowing in opposite directions then cause the storm cluster to start spinning and the rising warm air causes pressure to decrease at higher altitudes. The air rises faster and faster to fill this low pressure, in turn, drawing more warm air off the ocean surface and sucking cooler, drier air downwards. As the storm travels over the ocean it starts to pick up more warm, moist air, and wind speeds accelerate as more and more air is being sucked into the low pressure centre. A fully-formed storm can take anything from several hours to a few days to form and is comprised of an eye of calm wind and low pressure at the centre, surrounded by a spinning vortex of high winds and intense rainstorms.

C

The Saffir-Simpson scale is used to categorise hurricanes, especially in the Americas and increasingly throughout the rest of the world. Category 1 storms are the weakest, registering wind speeds of 74-95mph. These systems are unlikely to cause serious damage or widespread flooding, producing a storm surge of just 1.2 to 1.5 metres above normal. Category 2 storms have slightly more serious implications. Wind speeds can range from 96 to 110mph, strong enough to cause slight damage to roofs, as well as compromising the integrity of weaker trees and building structures. The storm surge produced is about 1.8 to 2.4 metres, which is still not enough to cause any major flooding.

D

Category 3 hurricanes are much more problematic and produce wind speeds (111 to 130mph) capable of causing more serious damage to building structures in general and localised severe flooding, with a storm surge of 2.7 to 3.7 metres. Category 4 systems are extremely dangerous and pose a serious threat to human life. Wind speeds of 131 to 151mph destroy whole roofs and cause major structural damage to entire buildings. A storm surge of 4 to 5.5 metres increases the likelihood of more widespread flooding, too.

E

The largest storms, Category 5, can bring devastation and pose an immediate threat to human life where they make landfall. Winds speeds upwards of 151mph have the capacity  to raze entire buildings. A storm surge of 5.5 metres or more is typically produced and not only is there localised flooding in the immediate vicinity of the location where the hurricane makes landfall, there is also widespread, serious flooding further inland.

F

Hurricane Danny is a Category 1 storm which made landfall near Lake Charles, Louisiana in 1985. As it tracked across the Atlantic towards America, the system appeared to pose little threat until it suddenly intensified into a tropical storm and then a hurricane in the space of 24 hours on the 14th of August that year. Danny's wind speeds were not significant enough to pose a serious threat when the storm made landfall and it quickly weakened into a tropical depression again. The real danger posed by systems of this kind is the potential for heavy rainfall; Danny dropped three inches over Louisiana in the space of a few hours. The other major risk factor is the threat of tornadoes spouting. Danny produced 14 tornadoes, a record for any hurricane at that time, which were responsible for several fatalities and caused over $100 million worth of damage.

G

Hurricane Andrew is a Category 5 storm at the other end of the scale which struck the Florida coast on August 24th 1992. Unlike Danny and most hurricanes, this storm system was directly responsible for causing widespread damage. It was the intensity of the winds rather than the volume of rainfall, flooding or offshoot tornadoes which wreaked the most havoc. Peak wind speeds of 165mph flattened outbuildings and prefabricated houses, and levelled entire neighbourhoods across Miami. 25% of the trees in the Florida Everglades were knocked down in the storm and upwards of $26 billion dollars of damage was caused, making it the second-costliest hurricane in U.S. history.

H

Every intense depression brings its own unique set of challenges. Hurricane Katrina, which made landfall in Louisiana in the summer of 2005, was the costliest and one of the deadliest storms in American history, yet it was only a Category 3 event when it struck New Orleans. Katrina illustrates that it is not just the intensity of the storm which determines its capacity for destruction, but also other factors such as the preparedness of the people in its path and the geographic features of the land (height above sea level etc.).

Questions 1-4

Complete the table below.
Write NO MORE THAN TWO WORDS for each answer.

Category:	1	2	3	4	5
Wind Strength	speeds of up to 95mph	speeds range from 96 to 110mph	111 to 130mph wind speeds	wind speeds of 131 to 151mph	wind speeds in excess of 151mph
Potential Consequences	only minor 1 _____ likely and probability of widespread flooding very low	slight roof damage and potential to threaten stability of weak trees and building structures	may cause slightly more serious structural damage to buildings, isolated cases of serious 3 _____ also likely	entire roofs may be destroyed and buildings may be subject to major structural damage, higher probability of widespread flooding	flooding in coastal areas and 4 _____ , entire building structures may be compromised
Effect on Sea Level	likely to rise up to 1.5m higher than normal	a surge of between 1.8 and 2.4m is 2 _____	storm surge of 2.7 to 3.7m	surge of 4 to 5.5m	surge in excess of 5.5m

TASK INFORMATION: LOCATING INFORMATION

This task requires you to scan the text to find specific information in a paragraph.

You must:
- (i) read a text divided into labelled paragraphs.
- (ii) read statements which focus on details contained within a paragraph.
- (iii) find which paragraph contains the information in each statement.

Questions 5-13
*Sample Reading Passage 7 has eight paragraphs, **A-H**.*
Which paragraph contains the following information.

5. factors other than the actual strength of the hurricane play a part in determining its destructive capacity _____

6. the majority of hurricane systems are not the direct cause of the destruction they bring _____

7. a storm that grew in strength in a very short space of time _____

8. there is no global convention for how to measure or categorise hurricanes _____

9. hurricanes are relatively tame at their centre, which is encircled by spiralling winds _____

10. intense storm systems are called different names dependent on where they occur _____

11. a storm that caused damage disproportionate to its intensity _____

12. a storm which was directly responsible for widespread destruction _____

13. winds that blow a regular course have a role to play in the formation of hurricanes _____

Remember:
- Some paragraphs may contain the answers to more than one question; others may contain no answers.
- The answers may be found in one sentence or phrase in the right paragraph or you may need to read more than one sentence

---

Method:
- **(i)** Look at the title or subtitle and decide what the text is about.
- **(ii)** Read the text very quickly to get a general idea of what it is about (read for gist).
- **(iii)** Read the first question carefully and find the part of the text which contains the same information as the question by searching the text for key words (scanning) or concepts (skimming).
- **(iii)** Check that the paragraph you chose as the answer has exactly the same information as the statement in the question.

TASK INFORMATION: DIAGRAM LABELLING

This task requires you to understand a detailed description and relate it to information in a diagram. Often, the text is concerned with a process or a description of something.

You must:

(i) scan the text to find specific information.

(ii) find one, two or three words or a number in the original text which fit suitably in each question gap and copy them into these gaps.

Sample Reading Passage 8

TORNADO THREAT

A

Tornadoes are among the most violent storms experienced on Earth. However, owing to the fact that the conditions necessary for them to form rarely exist, they are uncommon in most parts of the world. In the United States, however, in an area straddled either side by the Rocky and Appalachian mountain ranges, known locally as Tornado Alley, a frequent clash of cold airstreams coming down from Canada and hot air being pushed up from the Gulf of Mexico creates the perfect conditions for tornadoes to spout.

B

Tornadoes occur in the U.S. year-round with just under 20 reported on average in the month of January and almost 200 seen at the height of the tornado season in May each year. Winter storms are rarely very intense, but summer tornadoes frequently register an intensity of F3 or above on the Fujita Scale, the system used to classify the intensity of tornadoes. Though the scale is supposed to reflect the intensity of the storm, with F0 being the lowest intensity and F5 being the highest, it does not actually rely on wind speeds to determine its measurements. Instead, the convention is to base the rating of a tornado's strength primarily on the damage that it leaves in its wake - specifically, damage to human-built structures and vegetation. An F0 classification on the scale represents very light damage. An F3 is a severe event, while an F5 leads to widespread devastation. Wind speeds in an F5 tornado can be as high as 500km per hour and are capable of lifting strong-frame houses straight off their foundations and catapulting automobile-sized missiles through the air in excess of 100m.

C

Tornadoes form when a front of intense heat meets a block of cold air. The warm moist air explodes upwards, puncturing the layer above as it rises. A thundercloud starts to build and an intense, localised storm system, which may be accompanied by rain, thunder or lightning, quickly develops. The upward movement of warm air accelerates and can become very rapid. Winds from different directions then start to make it rotate. As this process intensifies, a visible cone or funnel drops out of the cloud towards the ground. If the funnel makes landfall, a tornado is born. These freak weather events can last from seconds to more than an hour and tornadoes have been known to travel over areas spanning several miles.

D

Before an imminent tornado strike, there will always be some telltale warning signs. The sky will have darkened considerably and may possibly even take on a dark-greenish complexion. There is often a hailstorm preceding a tornado and if the hailstones are unusually large, this is cause for heightened concern. A dark, low-lying cloud is one of the more obvious signs that a tornado is forming, especially if the cloud appears to be rotating. People often describe hearing a loud roar akin to the noise of a freight train passing by before a strike, too, which it is advisable to listen out for.

E

In order to have the best chance of surviving a direct hit by a tornado, it is essential to be inside a cement or steel-structure building. Mobile homes, trailers and vehicles do not provide adequate protection. Ideally, the basement or storm cellar would be the room of choice; however, in a building which has neither of these, the best option is to head towards the lowest and most central point, as far away from corners, windows, doors and outside walls as possible. Once there, it is best to be positioned under a sturdy table for added protection from flying debris and so forth, with the arms used to cover and protect the head and neck in particular. In the event that there is no form of shelter with the exception of a vehicle, mobile home or trailer, the best option is to abandon your cover and instead lie flat on the ground in a ditch or depression, hands covering the head for protection.

F

There are many myths surrounding the best way to survive a tornado, none of which contain even a modicum of truth. Opening the windows in your house will not reduce the amount of damage caused. It was thought by some that this would reduce the pressure differential between the inside of the house and outside; however, the differential is not great enough, nor does it last long enough, to be an issue in the first place. It takes on average 3 seconds for the pressure to equalise naturally in which time your house will not explode as people once believed would happen. Another popular myth is that sheltering under a highway overpass

will provide adequate protection from a tornado. In actual fact, research has shown that this could possibly be one of the worst places to be during a tornado strike for a number of reasons: (i) the ground under overpasses is often elevated above the surrounding land making it even more exposed, (ii) overpasses frequently collapse during violent storms and (iii) it is theorised that a wind-tunnel effect could occur in the shelter-area under the overpass. As a general rule, therefore, it is always best to follow the conventional advice.

Questions 1-5

Label the diagram below.
Write NO MORE THAN THREE WORDS for each answer.

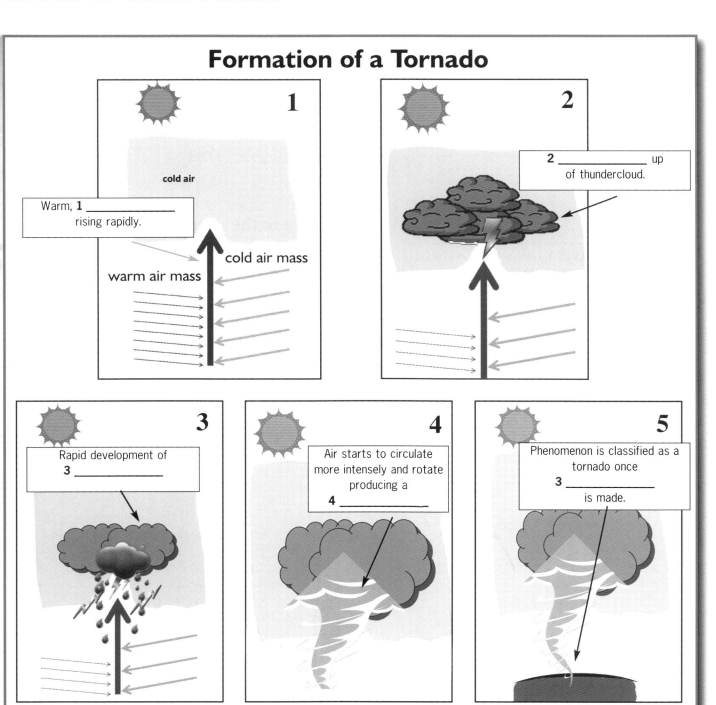

Formation of a Tornado

1

cold air

Warm, **1** _____ rising rapidly.

cold air mass

warm air mass

2

2 _____ up of thundercloud.

3

Rapid development of
3 _____

4

Air starts to circulate more intensely and rotate producing a
4 _____

5

Phenomenon is classified as a tornado once
3 _____ is made.

Remember:
- The answers are usually located in one or two paragraphs rather than spread over the entire text.
- The questions are not necessarily in the order the answers will appear in the text.
- Always look at the title of the diagram first; this will point you to where the required information might be located in the text.

Method:
- **(i)** Look at the instructions to confirm the maximum number of words you can write for each answer.
- **(ii)** Look at the diagram heading, read the questions, underline the key words, and decide what forms of words you will need for your answers i.e. nouns, verbs, adjectives etc.
- **(iii)** Identify the part of the text which you need and read it carefully (read for detail).
- **(iv)** Underline the words in the original text which fit the gaps and copy them in.
- **(v)** Read the diagram labels again to ensure that they make sense.

REVISION: FLOW-CHART COMPLETION

Questions 6-10

Complete the flow-chart below.
Write NO MORE THAN THREE WORDS for each answer.

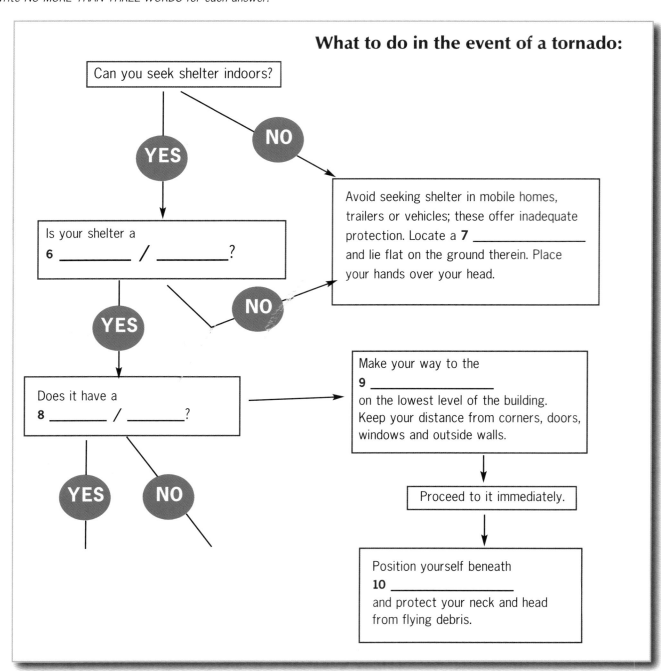

What to do in the event of a tornado:

Can you seek shelter indoors?

YES

NO

Avoid seeking shelter in mobile homes, trailers or vehicles; these offer inadequate protection. Locate a **7** _____ and lie flat on the ground therein. Place your hands over your head.

Is your shelter a
6 _____ / _____ ?

YES

NO

Does it have a
8 _____ / _____ ?

YES

NO

Make your way to the
9 _____
on the lowest level of the building.
Keep your distance from corners, doors, windows and outside walls.

Proceed to it immediately.

Position yourself beneath
10 _____
and protect your neck and head from flying debris.

REVISION: NOTE COMPLETION

Questions 11-13

Complete the notes below. Write NO MORE THAN THREE WORDS for each answer.

Tornadoes in America

- Parts of the U.S., collectively referred to by residents as **11** _____ , are affected by an unusually high number of tornado strikes.

- This is a consequence of cold and warm airstreams regularly interacting in an area which has **12** _____ on either side.

- The peak tornado season occurs every May.

- Tornadoes also occur in winter, though with less frequency - and they also tend not to be as **13** _____ .

READING SKILLS

There are four fundamental reading skills you will need to use in answering the questions in the reading test:

    (i) *Reading for Gist*   (ii) *Reading for Detail*   (iii) *Scanning*   (iv) *Skimming*

Reading for Gist

As a general rule, before your start to answer the questions associated with each passage, you should always *read for gist*. That means you should read through the passage quickly to get a general idea of what it is about. When gist-reading do not worry about individual words that you do not understand; focus on your general understanding of the text. Occasionally, it may be wise to read the questions before reading the passage. This is the case if the first task is a summary or note-completion type task, fo example. Reading the summary or notes may give you a general understanding of what the passage is about more quickly than if you were to gist-read.

Reading for Detail

This involves reading carefully and trying to understand the meaning of each point you read as accurately and fully as possible. You should not read the entire passage for detail, only sections in it which you have identified as being where the answers to the questions are located. To help you identify these areas, you may first need to skim or scan the text.

Scanning

Scanning the text involves running over it quickly with your eye in order to locate key words or phrases that you have underlined in the questions.

Skimming

Sometimes, because the questions have been paraphrased, the key words you have underlined will not be found in the text. It may then be necessary to search for key concepts instead; that is, sections of the text that talk about the information and ideas contained in the question using different words. Scanning is no good here as, well, the words are not the same in the question and text. What you must do then is skim; read very quickly from line to line trying to identify sections with similar content to the question.

Lead-In

A.

- At what age do you expect to retire?
- How do you expect your life to change once you have retired?
- Think about someone you know who has retired. Do you believe they have a good quality of life?
- Do you believe there are some jobs that are more suitable for younger people? Give examples and reasons for your answer.

B. Use the correct form of the words in the box to complete the sentences. All the words are connected to the theme of employment.

hire	appoint	agency	commission	dismiss
union	redundant	temping	applicant	salary

1. I decided to do some .... for a few weeks during the summer vacation.

2. Brian was .... because he was always late for work.

3. It took several days to interview all the .... for the job vacancy.

4. I signed up with the local employment .... because I couldn't find a job.

5. If you are made .... , you will be given an amount of money as compensation for losing your job.

6. If you belong to a(n) .... you can get free advice if you have problems with your employer.

7. I'm on a(n) .... of £60,000 but I pay a lot of tax.

8. We need to .... some more workers for the busy summer period.

9. When was he .... to the position of director?

10. I get 10% .... on every car that I sell.

Reading - 1

Pre-reading - Group work

A. Look at the words and expressions below which describe character and attitude towards work. Discuss what the words mean, and whether they are negative or positive. Use a dictionary to help you if there are words you don't know.

a high flyer ....

stuck in a rut ....

have a foot on the ladder ....

a go-getter ....

a bit of a plodder ....

unambitious ....

industrious ....

easygoing ....

competitive ....

ruthless ....

a team player ....

First Reading

B. First, look at the information below and decide if you think it is true or false. Then scan the text and see if your predictions were correct. Discuss any information that you find surprising with your classmates.

1. Future generations of Americans will probably retire at a younger age.

2. People tend to stay healthy for longer than they used to.

3. Older people are less active than they used to be.

4. Technology has made many jobs physically more demanding than they used to be.

5. Many people can't afford to retire early.

Living a Long and Prosperous life

The graying of the workforce is better news than you think. Emma Shulman is a dynamo. The veteran social worker works up to 50 hours a week recruiting people for treatment at an Alzheimer's clinic at New York University School of Medicine. Her boss dreads the day she decides to retire: "We'd definitely have to hire two or three people to replace her," he says. Complains Shulman: "One of my problems is excess energy, which drives me crazy." Oh, one more thing about Emma Shulman. She's nearly 93 years old.

Shulman is more than an amazing woman; she just might be the harbinger of things to come as the leading edge of the 78-million-strong Baby Boom generation of the early 20th century approaches its golden years. Of course, nobody's predicting that boomers will routinely work into their 90s. But Shulman - and better known oldsters like investor Kirk Kerkorian, 90, and former Federal Reserve Chairman Alan Greenspan, 83 - are proof that productive, paid work does not have to end at 55, 60, or even 65.

Rather than being an economic **deadweight**, the next generation of older Americans is likely to make a much bigger contribution to the economy than many of today's forecasts predict. Sure, most people slow down as they get older. But new research suggests that boomers will have the ability - and the desire - to work productively and **innovatively** well beyond today's normal retirement age. If society can **tap** their talents, employers will benefit, living standards will be higher, and the financing problems of Social Security and Medicare will be easier to solve. The logic is so powerful that it is likely to sweep aside many of the legal barriers and corporate practices that today keep older workers from achieving their full productive potential.

In the coming years, more Americans reaching their 60s and 70s are going to want to work, at least part-time. Researchers are finding that far from wearing people down, work can actually help keep them mentally and physically fit. Many highly-educated and well-paid workers - lawyers, physicians, architects - already work to an advanced age because their skills are valued. Boomers, with a better education than any previous generation in history, are likely to follow that pattern. And today's rapid **obsolescence** of knowledge can actually play to older workers' advantage: It used to be considered wasteful to train people nearing retirement. But if training

has to be refreshed every year, then companies might as well retrain old employees as young ones. Equally important, high-level work is getting easier for the old. Thanks to medical advances, people are staying healthy, enabling them to work longer than before. Fewer jobs require physically demanding tasks such as heavy lifting and technology - from memory-enhancing drugs to Internet search engines that serve as auxiliary memories - will help senior workers compensate for the effects of ageing.

In part, of course, the latest uptick in working ages can be blamed on the stockmarket's drop from its 2000 peak, which severely **dented** retirement savings. Also, fewer workers have good defined-benefit pension plans, which would allow them to retire young. But financial need can't be the only reason older Americans are working more. Federal Reserve surveys show that older families have been getting richer, not poorer. The average net worth of families headed by 55 - 64-year-olds **soared** by 74% between 1992 to 2004, after adjusting to inflation, and likely has gone up even more since then. At least as important is the fact that many institutional barriers to working longer have been removed. In 1986, in the name of equal rights, Congress banned **mandatory** retirement for all but a handful of workers, such as airline pilots.

The Baby Boom generation is even fitter for its age and more determined to stay active. Two-thirds of the people surveyed last year by the Employee Benefit Research Institute, a company-backed organisation, said they expect to work for pay in retirement. A survey of boomers found that two in five workers aged 50 to 65 were interested in a gradual, "phased" retirement instead of an **abrupt cessation** of work - and nearly 80% of those said that availability of phased retirement programmes at work would encourage them to keep working longer. While it is likely that many boomers won't **stick to** those brave resolutions, it is clear that more and more older workers are tending to postpone their retirement, and this trend is likely to continue.

Second Reading

C. Using your own words as far as possible, say what the following numbers refer to in the text.

1. 78 million (para 2) _____

_____

2. 74% (para 5) _____

_____

3. 80% (para 6) _____

_____

D. Using your own words as far as possible, answer the questions by reading and interpreting the meaning of the text.

1. Why will Emma Shulman's boss have to hire more than one person to replace her when she retires?

_____

_____

2. Why is it still currently difficult for many older workers to reach their full potential?

_____

_____

3. Why does it now make sense to train older employees?

_____

_____

4. Give two examples of how technology has helped people to work for longer.

_____

_____

5. What, for many people, is a favourable alternative to sudden retirement?

_____

_____

Vocabulary in context

E. Find a word or expression in bold in the text that has the same meaning as (or a similar meaning to) each of the following:

1. compulsory; required   _____

2. something or somebody that is of no use but costs money   _____

3. the act of stopping or ending something   _____

4. start using a supply of something   _____

5. keep to   _____

6. to take from or reduce (an amount of money)   _____

7. in a creative and original way   _____

8. rise or increase greatly   _____

9. the condition of no longer being of any use   _____
   (and having being replaced by something better)

10. sudden   _____

F. Use the correct form of the words below to complete the sentences. All the words have been taken from the text.

veteran	recruit	harbinger	sweep aside
wear down	enable	demanding	enhance

1. Her looks were greatly .... by her new hairstyle.

2. He is a(n) .... of the Second World War.

3. All his fears were .... when he realised he'd passed the test.

4. We need to .... a manager to run the new branch.

5. Being a teacher can be a very .... job when the children misbehave.

6. He's been .... by her constant complaining and negative attitude.

7. This operation will .... you to walk again after a few months.

8. Analysts say the recent upsurge in spending is a .... of better times for the economy.

Class discussion

How effective is the social security system for elderly people in your country ?

UNIT 1 Reading

IELTS Exam Strategy

Skimming & Scanning

IELTS exam questions test many different skills. As a general rule, it is best to begin by skimming the text. Skim-reading involves reading the paragraphs quickly to identify the key themes and points of each paragraph, focusing on the first and last sentences of each and key words that are repeated throughout.

Once you have skimmed the text and gained a broad understanding of what is being discussed – the gist of the text – you should then look at the questions.

A useful technique to use when trying to find the answer to a question is to scan the text to find where the information relevant to the question is located. Scanning involves searching the text for key words or phrases. This method may help you identify the paragraph in which the answer is contained or indeed the sentence containing a relevant fact.

After you have scanned the text and found the part which relates to the question, it may be necessary to read this information carefully. Careful reading involves reading all the words slowly to ensure that you understand what is being said.

So, here's a good guide for tackling reading questions:
1) Skim the text for general understanding.
2) Scan for the section to which a question relates.
3) If necessary, read this section carefully to ensure your understanding of what has been written.

Sometimes you will be required to infer the writer's opinion. This means deciding what the writer's view is about something based on what has been written. Gist reading is very important here as it gives you an overall understanding of the piece and the writer's views. When answering such a question, it may be helpful to skim the text again. If the question is about the text as a whole, this will help you to answer it. If the question relates to the writer's view about a particular point in one of the paragraphs, locate the paragraph and read that paragraph carefully.

So, when asked to infer the writer's general view from the article as a whole, skim the text again to gain a general understanding and highlight areas where the writer's opinion is expressed. Read these carefully if necessary.

And, when asked for the writer's view on a specific point, locate the relevant paragraph and read it carefully.

Now, let's look at some questions based on the first text.

1: Multiple Choice
- The questions are in order, therefore the first answer will be found near the beginning of the text, the second answer next and so on.
- There are 4 choices – a,b,c and d. Choose the correct one.
- You may be given part of a sentence and asked to choose the best way to complete it or you may be asked a question, then you must choose the best answer.
- Sometimes there may be **more than four options** i.e. a,b,c,d and e and **two correct answers** – you will be told if there is more than one correct answer

After you have first skimmed the article to get a general understanding, scan for key words when answering questions 1-10 below. And remember, the questions are in the order the answers will appear in the text.

A. **For questions 1 to 7, choose the correct answer A, B, C, or D.**

Example   Emma Shulman
   A   is very easy to replace according to her boss.
   (B)   is almost 93 years old.
   C   has little or no energy to give to her job.
   D   is a candidate for treatment at an Alzheimer's clinic.

The correct answer is B.

1   What do many of today's economic forecasts predict?
   A Older people won't contribute much.
   B Older people will make a large contribution.
   C Economic collapse will postpone retirement.
   D Legal barriers will be hard to overcome.

2   What does research suggest about the effect work has on people?
   A It wears them down.
   B It causes health and fitness to deteriorate.
   C It can be beneficial to physical and mental health.
   D It makes them want to retire early due to stress and fatigue.

3   What group of people already tend to retire late?
   A boomers
   B those who do physical work
   C the poorly-paid
   D the highly-educated

4   Why does the fact that knowledge is becoming obsolete more quickly work to older people's advantage?
   A Because it is considered wasteful to train people nearing retirement
   B Because all employees have to be retrained every year, so age is not a factor anymore
   C Because older people are easier to retrain
   D Because high-level work is more difficult for young people

5   Technology aids the ageing workforce by
   A enhancing people's actual memory and providing auxiliary memory resources.
   B remembering the searches they conduct and sites they visit on the internet.
   C reversing the physical effects of ageing.
   D compensating for low productivity.

6   Pilots
   A may continue working after the normal retirement age.
   B received equal rights in 1986.
   C still have a mandatory retirement age.
   D joined Congress for the first time in 1986.

7   This article is about
   A competitiveness in the workplace between the old and young.
   B reasons for and advantages of older retirement ages.
   C the legal rights of older people in the workforce.
   D the problem of scarcity of skilled workers in some. fields

B. **For questions 8 and 9, choose TWO letters A-E.**

What **TWO** probable benefits will be gained if we tap into the talents of older people?

   A Living standards will be higher
   B Doctors will have less work to do
   C The workplace will be friendlier and more cooperative.
   D Problems financing healthcare and social security can be solved more easily
   E Young people will have more free time

C. **For questions 10, 11 and 12, choose THREE letters A-G.**

Which **THREE** of the following choices are reasons more people are retiring later nowadays?

   A Older families are getting richer.
   B People have fewer savings.
   C There are fewer legal barriers stopping older workers.
   D Older workers receive better pensions.
   E People no longer slow down with age.
   F Fewer workers have good pension plans.
   G They must adjust to inflation.

Vocabulary

A. Study the text to try to understand the meaning of the words in bold.

Life in the Fast Lane

In our modern, competitive world, employers are beginning to expect almost complete **devotion** from their employees. But what is it that is leading a growing army of workers to tolerate such heavy demands all for the sake of earning a little money? **Peer** pressure is certainly a part of it. **Incessant** media pressure has a lot to answer for too. We are **bombarded** by images of the latest products available to those who are in the right earning group and the fact that the majority of people use plastic to purchase goods these days is **indicative** of the 'spend now, pay later' culture that is **blighting** modern society and leading so many into debt.

The **prevailing** trend for young people to spend hours surfing the internet and the growing popularity of E-bay has made it all too easy for people to purchase expensive goods without really coming to terms with how much money they are spending. Perhaps, most at fault however, are the credit card companies and banks that permit and often **blatantly** encourage people to spend beyond their means. Once people are caught in this kind of financial trap, it is incredibly difficult for them to **extract** themselves from the burden of interest that must be paid on expensive loans and overdrafts.

So how can we learn to **evaluate** our life in a more constructive manner? There is a need to regain some of the basic priorities and values of the past. There needs to be a **shift** in emphasis from materialism to building and **maintaining** personal relationships, both within a close-knit circle of family and friends and with colleagues and associates. Welfare needs to become the number one priority in a world that is becoming smaller through technology. The global village needs to adopt a village mentality of caring by going back to the basics.

B. Complete the sentences with the correct form of the words in bold from the text.

1. If you can bear to .... yourself from that book for a moment, I would like to talk to you about something.

2. There seems to be a .... fashion for long hairstyles for men at the moment.

3. He .... stole the apple from the shop without appearing to be at all nervous about being caught.

4. Most people thought he was innocent when the case first began but there has been a recent ....
in public opinion and the majority of people now seem to think he is guilty.

5. It is quite difficult to .... the importance of his role in the company when he has only been working here
for a brief period of time.

6. His .... to his family is obvious because he puts them before anything else in his life.

7. The politician was exhausted after being .... with questions at the press conference.

8. This latest argument is .... of his negative attitude.

9. It's hard to .... a close relationship with someone that you do not see very often.

10. Your .... complaining is driving me crazy.

11. His chances of winning the competition were .... by a leg injury.

12. Teenagers are often influenced by the attitudes of their ....

Reading - 2

A. The subject matter of the text below is very similar to that of Life in the Fast Lane. Refer to the Life in the Fast Lane text to find the missing words which fit into gaps 1-9. Use **NO MORE THAN TWO WORDS** for each gap. The first one is done for you.

BACK TO BASICS

Much more is expected of company (0) *employees* today than in the past. The motivation for workers to put up with the ever-increasing (1) _____ of their employers is simply a desire to earn extra money; with the world becoming increasingly obsessed with material possessions, our cash-strapped consumption-driven society works longer and longer hours to fuel its penchant for spending. And even when we don't have the physical cash to pay for our purchases, we can satisfy our desire to have the latest products by virtue of our trusty credit cards. The only problem with this is that an over-reliance on credit is driving many people into serious (2) _____ .

The (3) _____ has made it even easier for us to purchase expensive goods, as now we can do so from the comfort of the sitting-room sofa. Banks and other financial institutions also facilitate our spending urges, and for doing this they are very much (4) _____ . It is now far too easy to get credit. On the other hand, once you've fallen into the (5) _____ of indebtedness, it is incredibly difficult to (6) _____ yourself from this unpleasant financial situation.

Clearly, however, it is not just the banks and credit card companies who are to blame; after all, we are the ones engaging in such self-destructive behaviour. Why work long hours and get yourself into debt? Surely this is not the formula for happiness. There is an urgent need for people to step back and (7) _____ their behaviour, and (8) _____ their focus away from the material back to the values of the past. What we have *IS* the most important thing, but not in the material sense; our (9) _____ with family and friends will define what we REALLY have - and when all our fancy purchases are old and rusting away in some dirty corner of the attic, or on top of the dump heap, our family and friends will be ALL we have left.

B. Complete gaps 1-6 in the flow-chart below. Use **NO MORE THAN THREE WORDS** from the text **LIFE IN THE FAST LANE** for each gap.

The Problems caused by being too focused on Material Possessions

Individuals are compelled to spend a lot of money buying the latest products thanks, to some extent, to pressure coming from both peers and the (1) _____ .

Employees (2) _____ a very heavy workload in order to earn more money to buy the latest products.

Individuals get easy credit from banks and (3) _____ to finance their purchases.

Apart from using their credit cards, individuals take out high-interest (4) _____ to finance their purchases.

Individuals struggle to maintain their quality of life, and (5) _____ with close friends and family suffer as a consequence of not being prioritised.

Individuals fall into a financial (6) _____ and become heavily indebted.

UNIT 1 Reading

C. Complete each of the proverbs with a suitable word from the box below.

will	haste	cloud	sight	eggs	milk
absence	charity	silence	honesty	minds	worm

1. It's no use crying over spilt ....
2. Every .... has a silver lining.
3. Don't put all your .... in one basket.
4. .... makes the heart grow fonder.
5. .... is the best policy.
6. More .... less speed.
7. Where there's a .... there's a way.
8. Great .... think alike.
9. Speech is silver, ... is golden.
10. The early bird catches the ....
11. Out of ...., out of mind.
12. .... begins at home.

D. Choose suitable responses to the statements below from proverbs 1-12 in exercise C, above.

1. Do you think I should admit that it was me who broke his camera?
2. John never writes to me now that he's moved to Canada.
3. I really don't see how we are going to get this project finished on time.
4. It's such a coincidence that we both bought tickets to the Bon Jovi concert.
5. I lost my job but I've been offered an even better one!
6. My heart is set on studying at that university; I haven't even applied anywhere else.
7. I just dropped my favourite vase.
8. The sales start tomorrow so I want to get to the shop first thing before it opens.

UNIT 2 — Art and Culture

Lead-In

A.

- In what ways do you think art can reflect a society?
- Do you believe good art has to convey a message or can it just be pleasing to look at?
- Do you think art can influence the way people feel about things?

B. Use the correct form of the words in the box to complete the sentences. All the words are connected to the theme of art.

commission	vivid	restorer	figurative
forger	taste	patron	trace
etch	easel	composition	pose

1. This painting has a strange .... as the people are sitting on top of the house.
2. The glassmaker .... the design onto the glass.
3. We will need to take the damaged painting to a ....
4. The model stood very still as he .... for the artist.
5. I like .... paintings much more than abstract art.
6. Lord Brandon is a .... of the arts as he pays local artists to make art for his large house.
7. We have decided to .... an artist to paint our child's portrait.
8. The child .... the picture of the cat through transparent paper because it was too difficult to draw.
9. The .... was arrested by the police after trying to sell a fake painting.
10. I like this painting because the colours are so .... and it makes me happy.
11. The artist put the painting on the .... while he worked on it.
12. It's all a matter of .... when it comes to choosing the kind of art you would like for your house.

Reading - 1

Pre-reading - Group work

A. Look at the adjectives in the box below. Put the words into two categories; (A) positive adjectives for describing a painting and (B) negative adjectives for describing a painting. Use a dictionary to help you if necessary.

vibrant	bland	graphic	unremarkable
gloomy	original	depressing	thought-provoking
sinister	expressive	evocative	cheery
uninspiring	captivating	striking	eye-catching
colourful	outdated	dark	dramatic
unique	unoriginal	dull	uplifting
tasteless	tired	forgettable	

(A) Positive Adjectives	(B) Negative Adjectives

B. Look at the paintings below. First, say what you think about each one and then choose your favourite and least favourite painting, explaining your decision.

First Reading

C. Scan the text to find the information.

1. When and where was art first exhibited at the Olympic Games?
2. How many artists submitted their work to the Paris Olympics?
3. What was the required subject matter for art shown at the Olympic Games?
4. Why is the composer Stravinsky mentioned in the text?
5. Who was Georges Hohrod?

Art at the Olympic Games

With the founding of the International Olympic Committee (IOC) in 1894, and the celebration of the first modern Olympic Games, French aristocrat Baron de Coubertin saw his vision - men being educated in both mind and body, and competing in sport rather than war - fulfilled. One of his other desires was to combine both sport and art, and he thus considered including artistic competition in the Olympic Games.

In May 1906, Baron de Coubertin organised a meeting in Paris for both IOC members and representatives of organisations of artists. The meeting ended with a proposal to the IOC to organise artistic competitions at the Olympic Games in five areas (architecture, literature, music, painting and sculpture). The works of art entered had to be inspired by sports. Preparations got **underway** to hold such competitions at the 1908 Summer Olympics, which were scheduled to take place in Rome, Italy. But the Italian Olympic organisers faced unexpected financial problems and were soon forced to halt preparations for the games, which the IOC then awarded to London instead. Initially, the British organisers were committed to holding the art competitions, but because of the limited amount of time available in which they had to get ready for the games, they were eventually forced to abandon the idea and focus only on the main Olympic events. The organisers felt that the artists would not have had enough time to prepare and submit their work.

Pierre de Coubertin was not discouraged, and sought to include the artistic events in the programme of the 1912 Summer Olympics, to be held in Stockholm, Sweden. Although the Swedes initially objected, opposing the idea of art combined with competition, they eventually gave in. The number of entrants was rather disappointing though; only 35 artists are known to have sent in their submissions. Nonetheless, gold medals were awarded in all five categories.

When the first post-war Olympic Games were held in war-**ravaged** Belgium, art contests were again on the programme, although they were little more than a **sideshow**. The 1924 Summer Olympics in Paris were different, however. The contests were taken seriously for the first time, and 193 artists submitted samples of their work. Remarkably, this figure also includes three Soviet artists, even though the Soviet Union did not officially take part in the Olympic games, at that time, viewing it as nothing more than a "bourgeois" festival.

The growth continued at the 1928 Amsterdam Olympics, where over 1,100 works of art were exhibited in the Municipal Museum, not including the submissions in literature, music and architecture. Artists were allowed to sell their works at the close of the exhibition, which was rather controversial given the IOC's amateurism policy, which required all competitors to be amateurs. In Amsterdam, four of the original five recognised fields of art were also subdivided into additional categories, creating several new events for artists to compete in.

On account of economic problems and the host city, Los Angeles, being so far away from Europe, participation in the athletics events of the 1932 Games was lower than it was in 1928. The art competition did not suffer in the same way, however, and the number of art works entered remained **stable**. The exhibition drew 384,000 visitors to the Los Angeles Museum of History, Science and Art. Art contests were also held in the Berlin (1936) and London (1948) Games, with reasonable success, although the number of entered works had significantly dropped by 1948.

From 1912 to 1948, although some of the art competitions' rules varied from Games to Games, the **core** of the rules remained the same. All of the entered works had to be inspired by sport, and had to be original (that is, not published before the competition). Like in the athletics events at the Olympics, gold, silver and bronze medals were awarded to the highest-ranked artists, although not all medals were awarded in each competition. On a few occasions, no medals were in fact handed out at all. Generally, artists were allowed to enter multiple works, although the exact number was sometimes restricted. This made it possible for an artist to win multiple prizes in a single competition.

In 1949, a report was presented at the IOC meeting in Rome which concluded that practically all contestants in the art competitions were professionals, and that the competitions should therefore be abolished, and replaced with an exhibition without awards or medals. This sparked a **heated** debate within the IOC. At a 1951 meeting, the IOC decided to reinstate the competitions for the 1952 Olympics in Helsinki. However, the Finnish organisers claimed there was **insufficient** time, and, in the end, neither an art competition nor an exhibition was held.

The issue continued to be debated within the Olympic Movement, and at the 49th IOC Session in Athens, 1954, the IOC members voted to replace the art contests with an exhibition for future Olympics. Several attempts have since been made to reinstate them, but without success. The Olympic Games continue to be connected with art exhibitions however. The Olympic Charter requires organisers of the Olympic Games to include a programme of cultural events, to "serve to promote harmonious relations, mutual understanding and friendship among the participants and others attending the Olympic Games".

While several of the Olympic art medallists have achieved at least national fame, few of them can be considered well-known artists **globally**. In fact, the 1924 Games featured better known jury members than entrants, with artists like Selma Lagerlof and Igor Stravinsky judging the works. Two presidents of the IOC have also been among the entrants in the Olympic art competitions. In 1912 Pierre de Coubertin, under the **pseudonym** "Georges Hohrod and Martin Eschbach", entered 'Ode to Sport', which won the gold medal. Avery Brundage, who competed as an athlete at the 1912 Games, entered literary works at the 1932 and 1936 Olympics, earning an honorary mention in 1932. He would later serve as the IOC's president from 1952 to 1972.

Second Reading

D. Choose the correct answer A, B ,C or D to answer the questions.

1 Pierre de Coubertin
   A. thought that athletes should also try to be artists.
   B. was probably a pacifist.
   C. was both an artist and an athlete.
   D. refused to fight in the war because he was an athlete.

2. For the 1912 Olympic Games, the host country
   A. was reluctant to have an art competition.
   B. refused to have an art competition.
   C. was not asked to hold an art competition.
   D. had more artists entered than any other country.

3. What did some people object to in the 1928 art
contest?
   A. The fields of art were further divided.
   B. There were not enough artists taking part.
   C. The artists could sell their artwork afterwards.
   D. None of the artists were amateurs.

4. The 1932 Games' art contest
   A. had fewer entrants than previous games.
   B. suffered due to financial problems and location.
   C. took place during a period of increased prosperity.
   D. had more artists taking part than athletes.

5. What change eventually took place in the Olympics?
   A. Professional artists were excluded.
   B. Art could no longer be exhibited.
   C. Art competitions were no longer judged Olympic events.
   D. IOC members could no longer submit art.

**E. Using your own words as far as possible, answer the questions by reading and interpreting
the meaning of the text.**

1. What was de Coubertin's ideal?
_____
_____

2. How important were the art competitions in the Olympic Games in Belgium?
_____
_____

3. What was the reaction to the 1949 report?
_____
_____

4. How was it possible for an artist to win more than one prize?
_____
_____

5. Were the Games beneficial for an artist's international reputation?
_____
_____

Vocabulary in context

F. Find a word or expression in bold in the text that has the same meaning as (or a similar meaning to) each of the following:

1. consistent; constant; unchanging   _____

2. something that is insignificant or unimportant compared to other things around it   _____

3. typically middle class or capitalist   _____

4. already happening   _____

5. main part of something; basis; center   _____

6. false name   _____

7. damage something so badly that it is almost destroyed   _____

8. emotional; causing strong feelings   _____

9. all over the world   _____

10. not enough; inadequate   _____

G. Use the correct form of the words below to complete the sentences. All the words have been taken from the text.

halt	seek	submit	drop	abolish	spark	reinstate	promote

1. You must .... your application by the end of the week.

2. News of their affair has .... a political scandal.

3. Slavery was finally .... after hundreds of years of racial and ethnic abuse.

4. After being unfairly dismissed, the man was .... to the position of supervisor.

5. The number of students applying for this college has .... since the new university opened nearby.

6. The policy of the government is to .... higher education for all young people.

7. The police had to .... the traffic to deal with the accident.

8. He has always .... to help other people with the large amount of money he makes.

Class discussion

Do you think the ideal of the Olympic Games representing the best of amateur athletics has been lost?

Exam Strategy

Classification:
This type of task requires the candidate to classify events, characteristics or pieces of information in the passage into given categories; for example, events could be classified into historical periods, characteristics into age groups etc. Note that the items to be classified will form a coherent set – the grouping will make sense and will be logically linked.

This is testing your ability to recognise relationships and connections between facts in the passage.

You should follow the advice given in Unit 1. Skim the passage first to get the gist of it and understand what the passage is broadly about. Then scan the passage to identify relevant information and read for detail if necessary.

In the questions below you will be asked to classify events into certain historical periods. There are more events than historical periods, therefore more than one event may be classified into each period.

Periods in Olympic History			
A: 1890 – 1910	**B: 1911 – 1930**	**C: 1931 – 1950**	**D: 1951 – 1980**

Period

1: Avery Brundage served as the IOC's president. _____

2: Pierre De Coubertin won the gold medal for his entry 'Ode to Sport'. _____

3: IOC members voted to include an exhibition of art at future Olympic events. _____

4: The International Olympic Committee was founded. _____

5: The organisation of artistic events at the Olympic Games was first proposed. _____

6: Only 35 artists submitted works of art for the summer games. _____

7: The 49th IOC Session took place in Athens. _____

8: A report was presented to the IOC stating all artistic entrants to the games that year were professionals. _____

9: Because of financial trouble in Italy, the summer games were awarded to London. _____

10: The artist contestants were taken seriously for the first time at the Paris games. _____

11: The IOC decided to reinstate the artistic competitions for the Helsinki Olympics. _____

12: Over a thousand works of art were exhibited for the first time. _____

13: Three Soviet entrants took part in the artistic events despite the Soviet Union's official stance of boycotting the Olympics. _____

Vocabulary

A. Study the text to try to understand the meaning of the words in bold.

American Abstract Expressionism

Abstract Expressionism was an American post-World-War-II art movement. It was the first specifically American movement to achieve worldwide influence and also the one that put New York City at the centre of the art world, a role **formerly** filled by Paris. The term was first **applied to** American art in 1946 by the critic Robert Coates. Technically, its most important **predecessor** is often said to have been Surrealism, with its emphasis on spontaneous creation. Another important **manifestation** of what came to be Abstract Expressionism is the work of American northwest artist Mark Tobey, especially his "white writing" canvases that, though generally not large in **scale**, anticipate the 'all over' look of Pollock's drip paintings. Jackson Pollock's famous technique, dripping paint onto a canvas laid on the floor, has its **roots** in the work of Max Ernst.

The movement gets its name because of its reputation for combining the emotional **intensity** and self-expression of the German Expressionists with the anti-figurative aesthetic of the European abstract schools such as Futurism, the Bauhaus and Synthetic Cubism. Additionally, it has an image that is rebellious, anarchic, highly idiosyncratic and, some feel, rather nihilistic.

In practice, the term is used to describe any number of artists working in New York who had quite different styles, and it is even applied to work which is neither especially abstract nor expressionistic. That said, Abstract Expressionist painters do tend to share certain definite characteristics, such as a **fondness** for large canvasses, an emphasis on the canvas's **inherent** flatness, and an 'all-over' approach, in which all areas of the canvas are treated with equal importance (as opposed to the center being of more interest than the edges, for example).

As the first truly original school of painting in America, Abstract Expressionism demonstrated the **vitality** and creativity of the country in the post-war years, as well as its ability and need to develop an aesthetic sense that was not **constrained** by the European standards of beauty.

The style attracted the attention, in the early 1950s, of the CIA. They saw it as a **means** of promoting the idea that the USA was a **haven** for free thought and free markets, and also as a means of challenging both the art movement of socialist realism **prevalent** in communist nations, and the dominance of the European art markets.

By the 1960s, the movement's impact was no longer so profound, given that abstract expressionism had been **assimilated** into the mainstream, yet its methods and followers remained highly influential figures in art and **profoundly** influenced the work of many artists who followed.

B. Complete these statements with the correct form of one of the words in bold in the text.

1. The artist had a great .... for this area as he loved to paint the landscape here.

2. Young children are full of .... and so can enjoy life to the full.

3. The name, 'Tornado' was .... the athlete because he could run so fast.

4. Working at the weekends is just a(n) .... of paying for my college fees.

5. He was .... the manager of a large hotel before he took this job.

6. Sadly, poverty is .... in this area.

7. He paints with such .... that no one dare disturb him when he's working.

8. This music has its .... in the Blues music of New Orleans.

9. The artist had gained a reputation for producing paintings which were not just enormous in ....,

   but equally so in visual impact.

10. As a young artist she was .... affected by Picasso's work.

11. His wild imagination was .... by the traditional teaching at the Academy.

12. The new teacher is not as popular as his .... was.

13. The factory had to .... the new techniques quickly in order to boost production.

14. Hospitality to strangers is .... in the character of the Greek people.

15. These large paintings are a(n) .... of the artist's passion for the sea.

16. This area is a(n) .... for wild birds as there are no roads or buildings nearby.

Idioms and expressions connected with colours.

C. Use words connected to colours to complete the sentences below.

1. Telling him that he played badly was like waving a .... rag to a bull as he was already in a bad mood.

2. Brian will be .... with envy when he sees your new car.

3. You are as .... as a sheet. Do you feel ill?

4. I feel a bit .... today as my friends have gone on vacation and I am stuck at work.

5. As it's your birthday tomorrow, we should go out and paint the town ....

6. You are too .... to jump into the deep end of the pool. You big baby!

7. He always sees life through .... coloured glasses because he's such an optimist.

8. My bank balance is in the .... again. I need to deposit some money quickly.

9. He's a bit .... behind the ears, but he'll soon gain experience.

10. Larry already has a nice house; he only says he wishes he had one like Tom's, because the grass is

    always .... on the other side.

Reading

Reading - 2

Look at the text below, _The Louvre_. Although it is a large text, Exercise D does not require you to read through and fully understand it. Instead, your ONLY task is to find the four pieces of information needed to label the diagram AS QUICKLY AS POSSIBLE. Read the instructions for Exercise D, and then skim (reading very quickly) or scan (look for key words or phrases) the text to locate the information you need. Read that information carefully if necessary to make sure you have the right answer. Try to finish before your classmates - this is a TEST OF SPEED.

THE LOUVRE

The Musée du Louvre, contained within the walls of the resplendent palace of the same name, is the most-visited art museum in the world, and a cultural landmark with which few people these days are unfamiliar. Each year it welcomes more than 8 million visitors through its entrance doors, many of whom flock to see the Louvre's stand-out attraction; the _Mona Lisa_, a Da Vinci masterpiece perhaps even more famous than the grand palace itself. Unsurprisingly, the most popular wing of the palace, the Denon Wing, is home to this and a number of the grand master's other works, notably the _Portrait of an Unknown Woman_. But Denon, the southern-most wing of the palace, is not simply an homage to the brilliance of Da Vinci; it also boasts a number of other highly impressive collections in its corridors, from 19th-Century French paintings to Italian, Spanish and Northern European sculptures, not to mention its Greek, Etruscan and Roman Antiquities collection, home to the famed _Venus de Milo_.

And that is what is so attractive about the Louvre; there is something amazing and utterly unique for the visitor to appreciate in almost every room and exhibition space. Indeed, since its grand unveiling in 1989, even the ground-level entranceway, with its steel-and-glass pyramidal structure, surrounded on all but one side by the main wings of the palace, has become something of an attraction in its own right. Originally a highly controversial addition to the palace, the pyramid seems to have been warmly received by foreign visitors and members of the French public alike, and, if anything, has made the Louvre a more distinctive cultural landmark than before.

In the Sully Wing, one of the world's largest collections of Egyptian antiquities can be found. This section of the building, which consists of four long, narrow, connected corridors, forming the shape of a rectangle, also houses decorative art exhibits from the 17th and 18th century, drawings and pastels dating from the 17th to the 19th century, and an array of Greek, Etruscan, Roman and Oriental antiquities. Sully also shares a collection of fine French sculptures (5th to 19th century) with the Richelieu Wing, into which its top-most corridor, following left, leads. Richelieu was once home to the French Finance Ministry, and it was not until 1993, marking the 200th anniversary of its opening, that the Musée Du Louvre finally had the entirety of the Louvre Palace devoted to the display of its exhibits, with the unveiling of the newly-remodelled and renovated Richelieu that November.

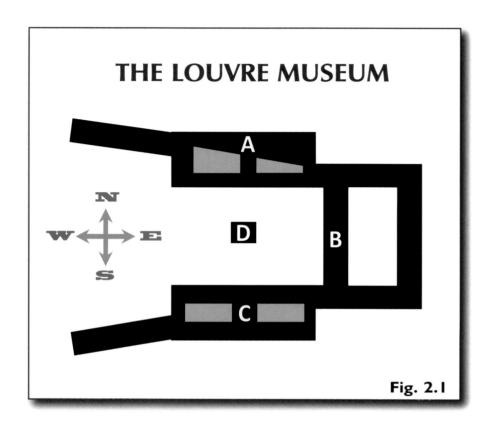

Fig. 2.1

Look at Figure 2.1. Four areas or wings of the Louvre Museum are labelled, **A - D**.
Using no more than three words for each answer, write the names of areas **A - D** below in answer spaces **1 - 4**. You will find the answers in *The Louvre*.

1: (A) _____

2: (B) _____

3: (C) _____

4: (D) _____

UNIT 3 [Around the World]

Lead-In

A.

 Where in the world would you really like to travel to and why?

● Can you think of a place that has a completely different culture from your own? In what ways would you say the culture of this place is different?

B. Use the correct form of the words and expressions in the box to complete the sentences. All the words are connected to the theme of travel.

backpacking	globetrotting	package	self-catering
culture shock	check-in	customs	in-flight
overhead locker	expedition	sights	tourist trap

1. We went on a bus trip to see all the .... in the city.

2. David has gone .... and is planning to visit every continent over the next year.

3. You must be at the .... two hours before your flight takes off.

4. The good thing about a(n) .... holiday is that everything is included in the price.

5. I like watching the .... entertainment when I fly to keep myself busy and not get bored.

6. I prefer .... accommodation because you can try out a different restaurant every night.

7. If the bag doesn't fit in the ...., you can't take it on the plane.

8. I'm going on a .... holiday so I can't take too many clothes with me.

9. They will check your passport when you go through ....

0. This is such a(n) .... that all the cafés can charge what they want.

1. I really suffered from .... when I travelled to India as everything was so different to what I was used to.

2. They have decided to go on the .... to the jungle to do some wildlife photography.

Reading - 1

Pre-reading - Group work

A. Look at the different types of holiday listed below. Discuss which would be your preferred type of holiday and why. What are the advantages and disadvantages of each of the different types of holiday listed

- an extreme sports holiday
- a package holiday
- a hotel/beach holiday
- a villa/pool holiday
- a cultural/sightseeing holiday
- a camping/hiking holiday
- an educational holiday involving a course in an activity like painting or cookery

First Reading

B. Read the texts about themed holidays and find which of the extracts mention the following:

1. a sunken ship
2. a choice of routes to follow on land
3. an early summer week of calming exercise in a hotel complex
4. a sport suitable for young and old
5. places where no one lives
6. somewhere where you need to wrap up warm
7. a place where you can acquire qualifications
8. fun in the evenings
9. introductory lessons before you go off on your own
10. something you can continue to do in your own home

Theme Holidays

A

From gentle cruises through **rural** villages to technical off-road challenges, get on your bike and head for the hills. With some of the finest trails around, mountain biking is becoming one of the popular holiday activities, and one which, as well as being fuelled by adrenalin, also brings the promise of lots of fun and adventure. For those keen to explore some of the best biking around, the Mediterranean is the best spot to get on your bike. With varied terrain, unique trails and a wealth of hidden places to discover, follow your guide and book into a group to experience two or three daily rides of various lengths and difficulties. With resorts offering guides fully trained by the Off-Road Training Consultancy, each ride will be clearly outlined with a description incorporating information on the final destination, trip duration, terrain type and level of difficulty – you simply select the ride for you. Head to Greece, Turkey or Croatia for a holiday experience you will never forget and come back feeling on top of the world with the added benefit of tightened and toned muscles! Included in the price of your holiday are a variety of high-quality mountain bikes to suit the local riding conditions around each particular centre, from leading brands Gary Fisher and Orange.

B

Without a doubt, this season has seen some of the best snow for years and with perfect powdery snow still present in all resorts, now is the time to catch a late deal. With resorts catering for all ages, levels and abilities, a ski or snowboard holiday may be just what you've always wanted but never dared to try. With fantastic mountain scenery, **revitalising** fresh alpine air, cosy bars and restaurants, lively après ski and endless non-ski activities, what are you waiting for? France and Scandinavia have both seen fantastic snow records this season and are good for late season bookings for families, groups and singles. If you decide to choose France, such is the great selection of resorts that you can be assured of finding the perfect one for you. Not to mention the fact that, just like the many professional skiers and snowboarders, from all over the world, who **head** to France each year in search of great powder, you, too, can enjoy some of the best terrain in the world. From the fashionable resorts of Val d'Isere and Meribel to the popular Chamonix and Les Arcs - the choice is endless. Scandinavia can be slightly chillier than some resorts in the Southern Alps but cold conditions mean good snow! Traditional and family-friendly, Norway and Sweden offer some of the best cross-country skiing, are great escapes from the most crowded resorts and are the place to come for unspoilt beauty and all-round winter activities.

C

If you fancy yourself as a bit of a 'sea urchin' then why not opt for a diving holiday? With year-round sunshine and warm water, Egypt is the only place to go. With a variety of choices from the superb diving opportunities in Sharm el Sheikh on the Red Sea to a diving centre in Dahab where a more varied choice of water activities is available, this is a water baby's haven. Sharm el Sheikh is situated on the southernmost tip of the Sinai Peninsula where the desert meets the ocean. A popular choice for sun-worshippers and divers, Sharm el Sheikh has established itself as one of Egypt's most fashionable beach resorts and **boasts** some of the world's most famous dive sites including the wreck of Thistlegorm, the Ras Mohammed National Park and the Straits of Tiran. Dahab lies at the foot of the majestic red tinted mountains of the Sinai and with a beautiful crescent-shaped bay, this is one of Egypt's quieter resorts. The activity centre in Dahab can offer a full range of courses from a PADI course for beginners to a PADI Divemaster. Combined with the other water-based activities on offer, this is pure adventure and relaxation rolled into one. Stay at the Coralia Club, a truly **spectacular** retreat situated at the lagoon end of the bay.

D

When messing around in the water and climbing the mountains gets all too much, then why not head back to town for some serious relaxation! Yoga is becoming more and more popular at home and abroad and with so many celebrities practising yoga in their daily routine, what better way to **chill** than with a bit of mental relaxation. A combination of physical toning and mental calming, yoga is accessible to all levels, regardless of age, fitness or flexibility. *The Retreat* in Sivota, Greece, makes a superb setting for unwinding and meditating and enthusiasts looking to maximise their yoga experience can book onto a Yoga Week from May 14th-21st. Located in a corner of natural beauty with tiny coves, green hills and deserted beaches, The Retreat clings to a coastal hillside, and with only 100 steps down to the waterfront you will be greeted by picture-perfect views. Rooms are housed in either the stunning main hotel or in one of the villa-style garden rooms - each room is linked to *The Retreat* by steps and paths.

E

If you have ever imagined yourself sailing the high seas on a 39ft boat, exploring Mediterranean coastlines and finding secret islands, then a sailing holiday may be for you. For some, yachting is all about new challenges and for others it's all about remote sandy beaches and **pristine**, clear waters. Traditionally, learning to sail a yacht has always been considered a rather long, drawn-out affair, but, in reality, sailing a flotilla yacht in the Mediterranean simply requires a practical understanding of sailing, an appreciation of basic navigation, some mooring skills and the ability to perform certain safety manoeuvres. Following an introductory course, days are spent cruising from bay to bay, mooring or anchoring in various locations with a small team of experts whose mission is to ensure you make the most of your vacation. The Dalmatian Coast in Croatia has a reputation for stunning scenery, reliable breezes and an abundance of sheltered bays and harbours. Made up of a dramatic string of islands, some with hidden villages - and many **uninhabited** - there are endless small bays and inlets with welcoming warm luminous sea. The coastline runs in a **predominantly** northwest-southeast direction with great cruising around unspoilt remote islands. The Croatian coastline is perfect for sailing vacations, and with so many islands and ports, you can stop as many times as you like for as long as you wish.

Second Reading

C. Choose the most suitable title for each of the five texts from the list **A-G**. There are two extra titles that you do not need to use.

1. Text A	**A.** Taking the plunge
2. Text B	**B.** Out on the crest of a wave
3. Text C	**C.** Adventure underground
4. Text D	**D.** Get into gear
5. Text E	**E.** Sit up straight and relax
	F. Hitting the slopes
	G. Beach sports galore

Vocabulary in context

D. Find a word or expression in bold in the text that has the same meaning as (or a similar meaning to) the following:

1. very impressive to see or watch _____
2. a word to describe a place in which no one lives _____
3. being in or of the countryside _____
4. has something that it can be proud of, or something that is special or unique _____
5. making one feel refreshed, relaxed and healthy again _____
6. relax _____
7. perfectly clean, unspoilt _____
8. move or travel towards _____
9. encourage, fill with, power _____
10. mainly, generally _____

E. Use the words below to complete the sentences. All the words have been taken from the text.

spot	duration	haven	wreck
manoeuvre	abundance	flexibility	cove

1. The divers found the .... of an old ship on the seabed.

2. This is a lovely .... for a picnic.

3. Athens has an .... of sights for tourists to visit.

4. This resort is a .... for families on holiday as it has everything they need and it is safe.

5. We moored the yacht in a sandy .... and went for a swim.

6. If you insist on going on holiday in August, you must have the .... to stay wherever we find a room.

7. For the .... of the exam, you must sit in silence.

8. It was quite a difficult .... parking the car in such a small space.

Discussion

Which of the holidays in the text would you like to go on and why?
Do you think any of them would be unsuitable for children or elderly people?

Exam Strategy

Exam Strategy

Choosing Headings for Paragraphs or Sections of a Text:

Candidates are given a list of headings, usually identified with lower-case Roman numerals (i.e. i,ii, iii etc.). A heading will refer to the main idea of the paragraph or section. Candidates must match the headings against the paragraphs or sections of text marked alphabetically. A text that contains clear paragraphs or sections with defined themes is normally used.

Note that there will be more headings than paragraphs, so some headings are incorrect and should not be used.

This task tests your gist-reading skills. You should skim the passage for general understanding and then read over each paragraph more carefully to ascertain its theme, if necessary.

Questions 1 – 5
This reading passage has five sections, A-E.
Choose the correct heading for each section from the list of headings below.

List of Headings	
i:	Healthy highs on two wheels
ii:	A chilly adventure
iii:	Cruising the Med
iv:	Cycling tours of Egypt
v:	A relaxation holiday in Norway
vi:	Unwind in Greece
vii:	Underwater adventures
viii:	Sailing on the Red Sea
ix:	Catch an early winter sports deal
x:	Relaxing cycling tours

1:    A : ____

2:    B : ____

3:    C : ____

4:    D : ____

5:    E : ____

Short-Answer Questions:

This task requires candidates to answer questions about details in the passage.
The instructions will often state 'NO MORE THAN THREE WORDS AND/OR A NUMBER' or sometimes 'ONE WORD' or 'NO MORE THAN TWO WORDS'.
If candidates write more than the number of words asked for they will lose a mark even if the answer is correct.
Note that hyphenated words (i.e. sun-worshippers) count for one word and contracted words will not be tested. The questions are usually arranged so that the answers appear in order in the passage.

You will need to locate and understand precise information from the passage. Scanning and careful reading are useful skills to employ here. First scan the passage to find the relevant information and then read it carefully to ensure that you understand.

Questions 6 – 10
Answer the questions below.
Choose **NO MORE THAN THREE WORDS** from the passage for each answer.

6: What aspect of the mountain-bike ride descriptions would probably be of most interest to a beginner mountain biker?

_____

7: What is located at the southernmost tip of the Sinai Peninsula?

_____

8: What can you catch this season due to the high amount of snowfall?

_____

9: What does Greece make a superb setting for?

_____

10: What is the Croatian coastline perfect for?

_____

> ### Identification of writer's views/claims or information in the text:
> This task type has two variations. The candidate will be given a number of statements and asked
> - 'Do the following statements agree with the views/claims of the writer?'   or
> - 'Do the following statements agree with the information in the text?'
> In the first variation, candidates are asked to write 'yes', 'no' or 'not given'. In the second variation, candidates are asked to write 'true', 'false' or 'not given'.
> It is important to remember that 'not given' should be used when information is neither confirmed nor contradicted in the passage. The student should base his/her answers on the information in the passage only and should not use his/her own general knowledge to answer the questions.
> For example, even if the student knows that a piece of information is true/false from his/her general knowledge, if this is not confirmed in the text, the answer should be 'not given'.

This task tests your ability to recognise opinions/ideas or particular points raised in the passage. Scanning should help you to locate the relevant part of the passage; you may also have to read carefully to identify the writer's views/claims.

Questions 11 – 14
Do the following statements agree with the information given in the reading passage?
> **TRUE**   if the statement agrees with the information
> **FALSE**   if the statement contradicts the information
> **NOT GIVEN**   if there is no information on this

		ANSWER
11	Mountain biking is becoming one of the most popular holiday activities.	_____
12	Egypt's year-round sunshine makes it an attractive water-sport destination.	_____
13	Norway and Sweden offer some of the best ski-jumping facilities in Europe.	_____
14	Sailing a flotilla yacht is very difficult and requires a great deal of training.	_____

Vocabulary

Vocabulary

A. **Study the text to try to understand the meaning of the words in bold.**

The new space tourists

Running out of exotic places to visit or more extreme thrills for an even bigger adrenaline rush? For those who can afford it, a **wholly** new travel experience is coming up over the horizon. When it arrives, space tourism will offer the **ultimate** in bragging rights. If things go as planned, flights into suborbital space ought to be more or less **routine** within three years - at least for those ready to **stump up** the $200,000 fare. But despite the price, the **jostling** to be at the front of the queue has already begun.

For that, thank Burt Rutan, the Californian aviation **pioneer** who won the $10m Ansari X-Prize in 2004 for launching his 'SpaceshipOne', a reusable rocket ship with a pilot and a payload equivalent to two passengers, into suborbital space twice within a fortnight. The object of the exercise was to prove that space flight could be done far more cheaply by private enterprise than by government. The $25m needed for Mr Rutan's privately financed space programme was put up by Microsoft billionaire, Paul Allen. This is about the cost of a pricey luxury yacht. Indeed, Larry Ellison, **founder** of the software company Oracle, paid **close on** $70m for a 244-ft motor-powered superyacht. That makes 'SpaceshipOne' look rather cheap.

'SpaceshipOne' is a rocket ship that's carried to a high **altitude** beneath the belly of a mother jet. Once it gets to the desired height, it is dropped from the mother ship and fires its rocket engine. The craft is what is known as a suborbital vehicle. This means it is powerful enough to climb through the Karman Line, an internationally **designated** altitude of 100km (62 miles) that **defines** the start of outer space. It cannot travel fast enough to go into orbit - the staging post for flight to the moon and **beyond**. But anyone who crosses the Karman Line experiences weightlessness, can see the curvature of the Earth below and the inky blackness above, and qualifies for **civilian** astronaut's "wings" from America's Federal Aviation Administration.

Out of the billions of people on the planet, very few have actually **ventured** across the boundary between the Earth's atmosphere and its surrounding space. In the four decades since the 'Apollo' and 'Soyuz' missions began, fewer than 500 people have become astronauts. Almost exclusively, they have been the super-fit and specially trained - and, **all bar** a handful, have been sponsored by the great powers of the world.

Apart from clinching the prize for the first commercial spacecraft, Mr Rutan won the admiration of millions of people on the ground. **Prominent** among them was Richard Branson, the British billionaire who founded Virgin Atlantic. As 'SpaceshipOne' touched down to **clinch** the $10m prize, Mr Branson was on hand to announce plans for a **fleet** of larger commercial craft based on Mr Rutan's design. Soon, the new service, run by Virgin Galactic, is planning to start giving fare-paying passengers the thrill of a lifetime.

B. Complete these statements with the correct form of one of the words or phrases in bold in the text.

1. We will be flying at an .... of 35,000 ft on this flight.

2. Billy wasn't brave enough to .... into the cold, deep water.

3. .... 500 people applied for the highly-paid position.

4. Some people believed that flying on Concorde was the .... experience in transatlantic flight.

5. Once the soldiers came off duty they couldn't wait to take off their uniforms and put on their .... clothes.

6. Mr Burgess is the .... of this company and through it he has fulfilled his career ambitions.

7. There will be a large .... of Russian ships in the harbour tomorrow.

8. This big banner .... where the race starts and ends.

9. Marconi was a .... in radio communication.

10. We had to work hard and negotiate for hours in order to .... the business deal.

11. I'm not sure that I .... agree with what you are saying.

12. Do you think you will be able to .... enough money for the new car?

13. The guests have returned from the walk, ... one who seems to have got lost.

14. This area has been .... as a pedestrian area so no vehicles are allowed here.

15. The scandal has been in the papers because it involves a .... politician.

16. The teenagers .... each other as they lined up outside the classroom.

17. From the hotel window we had a view of the mountains and .... to the sea in the distance.

18. Getting up at six o'clock every morning is .... for me now as I have to do it every day.

Phrasal Verbs 1

C. Complete the sentences with a suitable Phrasal Verb from the box below.

get away with	let down	fall through	stand in for
go off	put off	bring on	put up with

1. Why does he always .... us .... when we really need him?

2. I won't .... your bad behaviour any longer.

3. Our plans to go to Africa .... because we couldn't raise enough money.

4. What do you think .... his heart attack?

5. We'd better .... the meeting until next week if so many people are away.

6. I'll .... you if you want to take the day off on Monday.

7. How did he manage to .... a warning even though the police officer caught him speeding?

8. Don't drink that milk, it has ....

Phrasal Verbs 2

D. Complete the sentences with a suitable Phrasal Verb from the box below.

come up	pass out	pass down	run through
come up with	turn off	give off	turn down

1. I don't understand why she .... his invitation.

2. You need to .... at the next intersection.

3. Sorry I didn't meet you for coffee but something ....

4. The oven is .... a strange smell. Is something burning?

5. This painting has been .... from my grandfather, to my father and now to me.

6. He was so tired and hungry that he actually ....

7. Can you just .... the instructions with me again as I'm a bit confused?

8. He often .... a good idea when we don't know what to do.

E. Below are some of Burt Rutan's project notes. Fill in the gaps (1-6) in his notes using **NO MORE THAN TWO WORDS** from the original text *The New Space Tourists* for each answer.

Name of Project: **Spaceship One Outer Space Launch and Retrieval Programme**

Goal:
The **(1)** _____ of an independently-financed and built spacecraft into outer space and the returning of same craft to Earth, intact and capable of being reused.

Potential Reward:
(A) The first person/group to achieve the feat will claim the £10m Ansari X-Prize
(B) Success will generate a lot of commercial interest – already in touch with a well-known **(2)** _____ who owns a large airline company.
(C) Success also **(3)** _____ me to receive my 'wings' from the aviation authority.

Technical Target:
The **(4)** _____ of the craft must exceed 100km, the internationally agreed boundary between Earth and **(5)** _____ .

Financials:
The project is being **(6)** _____ by billionaire tech-industry magnate Paul Allen.

E. Below is a diagram showing the journey of Rutan's rocket ship into outer space. Fill in the gaps (1-5) using **NO MORE THAN TWO WORDS** from the text *The New Space Tourists* for each answer.

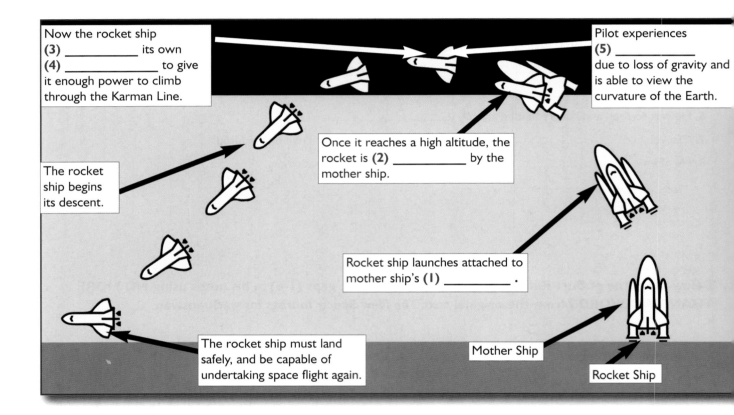

Now the rocket ship **(3)** _____ its own **(4)** _____ to give it enough power to climb through the Karman Line.

Pilot experiences **(5)** _____ due to loss of gravity and is able to view the curvature of the Earth.

Once it reaches a high altitude, the rocket is **(2)** _____ by the mother ship.

The rocket ship begins its descent.

Rocket ship launches attached to mother ship's **(1)** _____ .

The rocket ship must land safely, and be capable of undertaking space flight again.

Mother Ship

Rocket Ship

UNIT 4 [The Animal Kingdom]

Lead-In

A.

How often do you go for a walk in the countryside?
What species of wild animals can be found in the area where you live?
Are there any protected species in your country?
Are there any dangerous wild creatures in your country?

B. Use the correct form of the words in the box to complete the sentences. All the words are connected to the theme of wildlife. Use each word once only.

cub	**predator**	**fin**	**carnivore**	**pack**	**claw**
mammal	**migrate**	**poacher**	**scale**	**reptile**	**web**
herbivore	**stalk**	**herd**	**hibernate**	**prey**	**tusk**

Smaller animals have to be constantly on the alert for large .... that hunt them down for food.

The kitten scratched my hand with its sharp ....

When we went to our summer house for the first time, it was covered with spider ....

The lioness protected her young .... at all times.

Many small creatures .... during the winter months in order to keep warm.

The animals had been killed by .... who sold their fur illegally.

.... are creatures that give birth to live young and feed them milk.

The leopard .... the deer until it got close enough to attack.

Animals that are .... don't eat meat, only fruit, plants and vegetables.

10. Use a sharp knife to scrape off the .... before you grill the fish.

11. A .... of elephants slowly moved through the trees.

12. You can't feed the baby jaguar vegetables. It's a .... ; it eats meat.

13. Snakes and lizards are examples of ....

14. We knew there were sharks in the sea because we could see their .... sticking out of the water.

15. The elephants had been shot and their ivory .... had been cut out.

16. The lion followed its .... for several minutes before it attacked.

17. Many birds .... to warmer climates in the winter.

18. A .... of wolves roamed through the forest.

Reading - 1

Pre-reading

A.

● Do you enjoy watching nature programmes on TV? Why/why not?

● Do you think people are generally unaware of or unconcerned about the threat to wildlife caused by man?

First Reading

B. Read the text. Look at the questions below and choose the correct answer A, B, C or D.

Take a walk on the wild side

A   Most of wildlife watching is humdrum. Not dull - no, dear me, no. But you do need to find a different **mindset** if you want to get the hang of *it*. You need to make a mental adjustment. Many, many people turn to wildlife because they are inspired by the great and **gorgeous** images that flash across our screens at the touch of a button, by the endless **parade** of birth and death on the wildlife channels.

B   But this is not the same as watching wildlife. Let me start with a dramatic example. It's enjoyable to watch a documentary on lions - to see the great co-operative hunt; the kill; the **spats** around the carcass; the black-maned alpha male who hogs the meal alone but then (ahh!) permits one cub to share *it* with him. This is not the same as having eye contact with a lion. Amber eyes (with round pupils, too, like a person, not vertical slits like the cat on your couch) stare back with an easy **insolence**. You don't get that on the TV. You don't get the belly-clutch of fear.

C   But maybe that example was cheating - altogether too dramatic. What if you were to turn on the TV for a programme about lions and there weren't any? The narrator might say "Well, that's the way it is, but look, there are a few impalas, they're very nice, and listen, that's an orange-breasted bush shrike, and overhead you can see an eagle." That would make unwatchable television, but that's what watching wildlife in Africa is like most of the time.

D   When you take an aeroplane trip, the captain tells you to adjust your watch for the new country. When you go to look for wildlife, you must adjust your mind. You must stop expecting fights and scandals, lions and tigers, birth and death. You must start doing that thing we rarely do in modern life - living in the moment in which we find ourselves.

E   That's not mysticism; that's fieldcraft — mind you, it has a spiritually uplifting side as well. I remember researching a book about a bird reserve many years ago. On my research trips, I would spend, say an hour in a hide. This wasn't something I had done before. I had always believed that I lacked the patience for such a thing. The first five minutes were **enthralling**. Over the next ten minutes I would get bored and want to leave. But once I made myself stay, I found that an hour would go past almost without my noticing; so **absorbed** had I become in the humdrum doings of each moment.

F   When with tourists in Africa, the first thing I do is try to make them abandon their expectations that a day in the bush is like switching on the Discovery Channel. It's much better than that. It is now, it is you, and it is here. And totally unstructured. Thrilling things may happen, but then again, they may not. Isn't that more thrilling than certainty? So you learn to find a deeper way of understanding - and that's not about **rarities** and drama and brilliant views. It's about the humdrum pleasure of hearing a willow warbler, which is just as lovely in your local park as it is in the jungle. And it's the looking, every bit as much as the finding; it's the hearing, every bit as much as the seeing; and, perhaps **above all**, it's the glorious feeling that you are there and so are _they_. In Spain last autumn, I saw a paw print of an Iberian lynx. To be where a lynx was a few minutes before is a deep and glorious business, once you have learned to make that little adjustment.

G   I am not boasting here of my skill, of my knowledge, of my fieldcraft. All these things are poor. Rather, I have learned how to enjoy being where wildlife is and _that_, for most of us, is the most important field skill of all. People write about patience in wildlife watching as if it were a **virtue**. It is, in fact, a deep pleasure, a self-indulgence even.

H   People prefer to watch sport live because they don't know what will happen next, and that is exactly the same with wildlife, and perhaps with everything else as well. Life is best lived with an appreciation of the miraculousness of the ordinary. That law works for sport, for married life and also when you are looking at wildlife. True, you won't get the concentrated **blast** of non-stop action that you see on television, but what you do see, you will also live. That makes it a qualitatively different experience.

I   You have become less a spectator than a participant. You can, for example, spoil everything with inappropriate behaviour. You can in some circumstances put yourself in danger. The experience is **vivid** and ultimately irresistible. And here is the point of what I am saying: this is not a talent you are born with; we can all find it within ourselves. If I can, you can - if you haven't already done so. Knowledge helps, but even that is by no means essential. What matters is an easy willingness to make the most of things. You just set out with high hopes and low expectations. You live in the moment, and that enriches everything you see and everything you do - and the wonders will come of their own accord.

. What do wildlife programmes on TV tend to do?
A. Show how boring wildlife watching can be.
B. Sensationalise the daily activities of wild animals.
C. Only deal with dangerous animals.
D. Challenge the viewer mentally.

. What can TV not provide?
A. An interesting display of the lives of wild animals.
B. A true representation of the way wild animals live.
C. A feeling of real fear in the viewer.
D. Close-up views of the animals.

. Why does the writer compare being on a plane to wildlife watching?
A. They can both be quite frightening.
B. Many people have phobias about both experiences.
C. They both call for some kind of mental adjustment.
D. They are both potentially dangerous.

4. What does the writer say is the problem with tourists in Africa?
A. They cause a lot of environmental damage.
B. They want to be on a TV programme.
C. They disapprove of the way they are guided through the bush.
D. They have strong preconceptions about being in the bush.

5. In the writer's opinion,
A. we should stop trying to dramatise life.
B. we are no different to the animals that we see on TV.
C. it is better to live in the country than in an urban area.
D. in order to really appreciate wildlife you need to learn more about it.

Second Reading

C. Say what the following words in italics refer to in the text.

1. it (para A)
2. it (para B)
3. they (para F)
4. that (para G)

D. Using your own words as far as possible, answer the questions by reading and interpreting the meaning of the text.

1. What is the attitude of a lion in the wild when it sees a person?
2. What does the writer mean by 'adjusting your mind' in paragraph D?
3. What happened to the writer after he'd spent a long time in the hide?
4. What does the writer mean by 'humdrum pleasure' in paragraph E?
5. Why does the writer compare sport with wildlife watching?

Vocabulary in context

E. Find a word in bold in the text that has the same meaning as (or a similar meaning to) each of the following:

1. a quality someone has that is considered to be morally good
2. something that is not found or seen very often
3. very very nice, lovely
4. making a strong impression, having a great effect
5. a sudden, large amount of something
6. way of thinking, attitude
7. so involved or interested in sth that you are not aware of other things around you
8. very interesting
9. more than anything else
10. fight, argument
11. a lack of respect for sb/sth
12. a number of things one after the other

F. Use the correct form of the words below to complete the sentences. All the words have been taken from the text.

get the hang of	turn to	flash	hog	stare	switch on	set out	enrich

1. Don't .... the food, you aren't the only one who is hungry.
2. Good friends help to .... your life.
3. At first it was strange trying to ride a horse, but I soon .... it.
4. When I can't sleep I .... the radio and listen to music.
5. The fireworks .... across the sky.
6. He .... a life of crime because he had a drug problem.
7. We .... early in the morning so that we could get to the beach before it got busy.
8. He couldn't stop .... at the beautiful woman.

Exam Strategy

A. Locating Information:

In this task type, candidates are asked to locate specific information in the paragraphs of the passage, and to write the letters corresponding to the correct paragraph in their answers.

Candidates may be asked to find
- specific details
- an example of some kind
- the reason for an event, change etc
- a description
- a comparison
- a summary
- an explanation

Candidates will not always be required to find information in all the paragraphs; the question may relate to specific paragraphs. There may also be more than one piece of information in a given paragraph. In this case, candidates will be told they can use a letter more than once.

You should skim for gist to have a general understanding of the subject of each paragraph. You may then have to scan for specific information and read carefully for detail.

Questions 1 – 10

This reading passage has nine paragraphs, A-I. Which paragraph contains the following information?
Write the correct letter A-I in the answer section.
NB You may use any letter more than once.

	ANSWER
what watching wildlife in Africa is like most of the time	_____
the reason the writer believes many people turn to wildlife study	_____
the writer's surprise at his levels of patience	_____
the contrast between seeing big cat predators on T.V. and in the wild	_____
how we must adjust the way we think when studying wildlife	_____
the excitement of the uncertainty experienced in the bush	_____
the most important field skill in the writer's view	_____
the view that anyone can become a good nature observer	_____
the view that ordinary things can be wonderful when experienced firsthand	_____
0 how the writer felt when he saw the paw print of a lynx cat	_____

B. Sentence Completion:

There are two variations of this task type. **Type A:** candidates are asked to complete the sentence in a given number of words taken from the passage. **Type B:** candidates are given the first half of a sentence based on the text and asked to complete it from a list of possible options.

In Type A, candidates will be told in the instructions the maximum number of words that they can use to complete the sentence. The instructions for this type usually state 'NO MORE THAN THREE WORDS AND/OR A NUMBER', but sometimes candidates may be asked to write 'ONE WORD', or 'NO MORE THAN TWO WORDS'. Numbers can be written as figures or words.
Remember: do not exceed the word limit as you will lose marks even if you get the question right.
In Type B, candidates will have to choose the best option from a list. Candidates will have more options to choose from than there are questions.
If candidates are asked to complete a sentence, the words should be taken directly from the passage.

In both **TYPE A** and **TYPE B** questions, scanning is very important. Look for key words and phrases in the passage.

TYPE A:
Questions 11 – 12
Complete the sentences below. Choose NO MORE THAN TWO WORDS from the passage for each answer. Write your answers in the space provided.

11   When you are about to land in a new time zone, you must reset your .... , but when you look for

     wildlife, it is your .... that needs resetting.

12   People have a preference for watching live sport; the attraction surely being not knowing what is going to

     ....

TYPE B:
Questions 13 – 15
Complete each sentence with the correct ending A-F from the box below. Write the correct letter A-F on the answer line.

		ANSWER
13	People write about patience in wildlife watching	_____
14	Life is best lived with an appreciation of	_____
15	What matters is an easy	_____

A: the beauty of the wild.	**B:** way of finding the animals.
C: the wondrousness of the ordinary.	**D:** willingness to make the most of things.
E: because it is not so important.	**F:** as if it were a virtue.

Vocabulary

Vocabulary

A. Study the text to try to understand the meaning of the words in bold.

Wildlife in danger

The Great Bear Rainforest has been saved. Normally, when I hear news like that I **sigh** in disbelief. It's hardly ever true. 'Saved' usually means 'given temporary **reprieve**' or **merely** 'put on the agenda'. This time, however, I can't decide if I should be sighing or singing. The Canadian province of British Columbia has announced plans to protect a huge **swathe** of Pacific Coast rainforest - the largest tract of intact temperate rainforest left on Earth - and the newly-brokered deal will save about a third of this **vast** area specifically for wildlife.

I was in this wilderness of ancient trees, glacial waterfalls, rocky headlands, coves, inlets and bays just a few months ago. **Stretching** seamlessly from Vancouver all the way to Alaska, it is home to everything from bald eagles and beavers to wolves and whales. The highlight of my trip was an hour crouching almost within touching distance of a spirit bear, a rare white form of the American black bear, and one of the region's most famous inhabitants. It's an **exhilarating** place.

Conservation groups and First Nation communities have been fighting to protect the Great Bear Rainforest - which covers an area about twice the size of Belgium - since the late 1980s. After several premiers, **umpteen** ministers of the environment and countless presentations, meetings, books, reports, protests, blockades and arrests, the recent announcement is undeniably welcome news. Indeed, most conservation groups have been tripping over themselves to sing the government's praises.

But is protection of a third enough? What we're saying is that two-thirds of one of the most important wildlife regions on the planet is **up for grabs**. The agreement does specify that any logging and mining in the area must be sustainable, but anyone who believes that is **kidding** themselves. Canada's logging industry has an **appalling** track record.

The sad fact is that we've become used to losing environmental battles. Our expectations are now so low that we are thankful for progress of any kind. I'm not saying that every last tree needs to be saved, but perhaps we should **revert** to the days when we aimed a little higher.

B. Complete the sentences with the correct form of the words in bold from the text.

1. If he thinks he can get a good job without any qualifications, he is .... himself.

2. The desert .... from one side of the country to the other as it is so huge.

3. His behaviour was so .... that his parents were ashamed of him.

4. I've told you .... times not to do that.

5. John's car is .... if you are interested in buying it.

6. He was nice for a few days but then he .... back to his unfriendly behaviour.

7. Parachuting out of an aeroplane was a frightening but .... experience.

8. Bob .... sadly when he thought about the missed opportunity.

9. He .... asked if he could borrow the book and she shouted at him for no reason.

10. The Pacific is a(n) .... ocean that many sailors have tried to cross single-handed and failed.

11. At first they said we had to pay back the money immediately, but then they gave us a .... for a month.

12. The floods covered a huge .... of land and affected thousands of people.

C. Idioms and expressions connected to animals.

Complete each of the idioms or expressions with a suitable word from the box below.
Some of the words need to be used more than once. Use the correct form of the words.

fox	mouse	bull	chicken	fish
fly	cat	bird	dog	pig

1. Don't count your .... before they've hatched. You haven't got the job yet.

2. If you go to the post office after the bank you can kill two .... with one stone.

3. Don't worry about your girlfriend leaving you, there are plenty more .... in the sea.

4. Telling him that you have been promoted when he didn't even get a bonus was like a red rag to a ....

5. "He might help you on Monday." " Sure, and .... might fly. He never helps anyone"

6. You shouldn't have told Jane about the surprise party. You've really let the .... out of the bag.

7. The teacher told the children to be as quiet as a .... while they listened to the story.

8. Aren't you going to tell me where you've been? Has the .... got your tongue?

9. You need to take the .... by the horns and tell her how you really feel.

10. I'm sure it can't have been Billy that hit John as he wouldn't hurt a ....

11. I don't trust Susan; she's as sly as a ....

12. It's a .... life. All I do is work, work, work.

D. The text *A Cautious Welcome* was written in response to the Canadian government's pledge to preserve part of the rainforest. Fill in gaps 1 - 10 with a suitable word taken from the words in bold in *Wildlife in Danger*. Use each word ONCE only. You will not need all the words.

A Cautious Welcome

The temperate rainforests of Canada are not only **(1)** _____ in size, but similarly limitless in terms of the variety of animal and plant life to which they are home. News of a government-sanctioned programme to preserve them must therefore be welcomed, though it is disappointing to find out that only a **(2)** _____ of land running along the west coast, accounting for no more than a third of the overall forested area, will fall within the sphere of this preservation scheme. Indeed, it is **(3)** _____ to think what may become of the other two-thirds of this massive ecosystem, **(4)** _____ , as it does, all the way north to Alaska. Will it simply go the way of so many once-forested areas around the world and disappear into the footnotes of history? Indeed, the fact that so much of the rainforest is still in jeopardy despite this announcement makes one wonder whether the decision was political - **(5)** _____ a vote-grabbing exercise by the ruling party in government - or whether there is, truly, a commitment to preserve the land. There have been **(6)** _____ empty pledges by governments in the past, so you will excuse my natural scepticism. That said, if this government is being sincere, then I think I, and the rest of the environmental campaigners who have fought to preserve this **(7)** _____ , utterly enchanting place, will let out a collective **(8)** _____ of relief. If even an acre of rainforest were no longer **(9)** _____ , going to the highest-bidding greedy commercial forestry company, this would be a fact worth celebrating. So long as the government doesn't **(10)** _____ to type, therefore, and renege on its promise, this is very good news indeed - certainly a step in the right direction.

Reading - 2

Pre-Reading

A. First, look at the information below and decide if you think it is True or False. Then scan the text and see if your predictions were correct. Do any of the answers surprise you?

1. Dinosaurs are extinct and have left no descendants.

_____

2. For many years, scientists were mistaken about dinosaurs because of a single missing bone.

_____

3. It's now hard to decide where to draw the dividing line between dinosaurs and birds.

_____

Modern day dinosaurs

The origin of birds is a **contentious** and central topic within evolutionary biology. A close relationship between birds and dinosaurs was first proposed in the nineteenth century after the discovery of the fossil Archaeopteryx. To date, there is significant evidence that birds evolved from theropod dinosaurs and only a few scientists still debate the dinosaurian origin of birds; however, the exact ancestor that gave rise to the early birds within the theropods is still an unanswered question.

The primitive bird Archaeopteryx, from the Jurassic period, was discovered in 1861 in southern Germany, preserved in a rare and remarkable geological formation known for its superbly detailed fossils. Archaeopteryx possessed features clearly **intermediate** between those of modern reptiles and birds. Many consider Archaeopteryx to have been the first true bird, due to its feathered wings; however, Archaeopteryx could probably not fly and was limited to gliding from high places as it seems to have lacked the muscles required to move its wings upward.

Biologist Thomas Henry Huxley, known for his support of Darwin's new theory of evolution, almost immediately **seized upon** Archaeopteryx as a transitional fossil between birds and reptiles. Starting in 1868, Huxley made detailed comparisons of Archaeopteryx with various prehistoric reptiles and found that it was most similar to theropod dinosaurs. The discovery in the late 1870s of the iconic "Berlin specimen" of Archaeopteryx, complete with a set of reptilian teeth, provided further evidence. Huxley was the first to propose an evolutionary relationship between birds and dinosaurs, although he was opposed by some of his contemporaries.

Gerhard Heilmann, an artist by trade, also had a scholarly interest in Archaeopteryx, and from 1913 to 1916 published the results of his research in several parts, dealing with the anatomy, embryology, behaviour, paleontology, and evolution of birds. Like Huxley, Heilmann compared Archaeopteryx and other birds to an exhaustive list of prehistoric reptiles, and also came to the conclusion that theropod dinosaurs were the most similar. However, Heilmann noted that birds possessed collar bones fused together to form a bone called the furcula or "wishbone", and while such collar bones were known in more **primitive** reptiles, they had not yet been recognized in theropod dinosaurs. Since he was a firm believer in Dollo's law, which states that evolution is not **reversible**, Heilmann could not accept that collar bones were lost in dinosaurs and re-evolved in birds. He was therefore forced to rule out dinosaurs as bird ancestors and **ascribe** all of their similarities to **convergent** evolution. Heilmann stated that bird ancestors would instead be found among the more primitive reptiles. Heilmann's extremely **thorough** approach ensured that his book became a classic in the field, and his conclusions on bird origins, as with most other topics, were accepted by nearly all evolutionary biologists for the next four decades.

But contrary to what Heilman believed, paleontologists now accept that collar bones and, in most cases, wishbones are a standard feature not just of theropods but of saurischian dinosaurs. As of 2007, wishbones had been found in nearly all types of theropods. The fact that the wishbones were only recognised as such recently may be explained by the fact that they are relatively delicate bones and therefore in danger of being destroyed or at least damaged beyond recognition. Many were originally mistaken for ribs.

John Ostrom revived the link between dinosaurs and birds with a series of publications in the mid-1970s in which he laid out the many similarities between birds and theropod dinosaurs, **resurrecting** the ideas first put forth by Huxley over a century before.

In the 1980s, cladistic methodology, which involves statistical analysis of anatomical characteristics, was applied to dinosaurs for the first time by Jacques Gauthier and others, showing unequivocally that birds were a **derived** group of theropod dinosaurs. Gauthier came up with a long list of skeletal characteristics shared by these two groups, and not present in other groups, such as the presence of hollow, air-filled bones.

As modern-day discoveries reveal more non-avian theropods that are closely related to birds, the formerly clear **distinction** between non-birds and birds becomes less so. Recent discoveries in northeast China, demonstrating that many small theropod dinosaurs had feathers, contribute to this **ambiguity**. To date, fossils of more than twenty species of dinosaur have been collected which preserve feathers. This presence of feathers in flightless dinosaurs hints that feathers may first have evolved for warmth, or display. Another fossil, found in the early 1990s, was first thought to be a bird but was quickly recognised to be a theropod dinosaur. Surprisingly, its body was covered by long string-like structures. These were dubbed 'protofeathers' and considered to be primitive forms of the more advanced feathers of birds, although some scientists disagree with this assessment. Feathers or protofeathers have been found on a wide variety of theropods in China and the discoveries of extremely bird-like dinosaurs, as well as dinosaur-like primitive birds, have almost entirely closed the gap between theropods and birds.

First Reading

. Look at the following items (Questions 1-10) and the list of people below. Match each item with the person who first invented or used them. Write the correct letter A-D in boxes 1-10. You may use any letter more than once.

1. brought an old idea back to life

2. used statistics in his research

3. did not think birds evolved from dinosaurs

4. was an early supporter of Darwin

5. did exceptionally careful, detailed work

6. had largely unarguable results

7. was well respected for many years

8. was the first to suggest a bird-dinosaur relationship

9. used bones for his subject of study

10. worked in the 1970s

1.	
2.	
3.	
4.	
5.	
6.	
7.	
8.	
9.	
10.	

A. Huxley	**B.** Heilmann
C. Ostrom	**D.** Gauthier

Second Reading

C. Complete the table below. Choose NO MORE THAN THREE WORDS from the passage for each answer.

Animal Group	wishbone	teeth	body covering	flight	hollow bones
reptile	yes	yes	scales	no	**6** ....
1	yes	yes	sometimes **4** .... or feathers	no	yes
2	yes	**3**	**5**	gliding only	yes
modern bird	yes	no	feathers	yes	yes

Vocabulary in context

D. Find a word or expression in bold in the text that has the same meaning as (or is similar in meaning to) each of the following

1. from an early period of development
2. coming together; becoming similar
3. the quality of being unclear or confusing
4. causing disagreement
5. took great interest in
6. separation due to differences
7. done carefully so nothing is forgotten
8. may be changed back to an earlier state
9. one thing that is between two others
10. developed from something else
11. reviving; bringing back to life
12. put the cause of something down to

1. _____
2. _____
3. _____
4. _____
5. _____
6. _____
7. _____
8. _____
9. _____
10. _____
11. _____
12. _____

E. Use the correct form of the words from Exercise D above to complete the sentences.

1. It is said that whales once lived on land and their flippers are .... from arms and legs.

2. If you try this hair dye, remember it is not .... ; if you don't like it you'll have to wait until it grows out!

3. A new fossil was discovered of a(n) .... ancestor of humans.

4. Take either road; they are .... and will eventually meet up in the town's central square.

5. This coming season, fashion designers are expected to .... the styles of the 1950s .

6. The increased rate of lung cancer in women may be .... changes in smoking habits.

7. He's not a bad dancer but he still has a lot to learn; I suppose he's at .... level.

8. She saw a documentary about Madagascar and immediately .... the idea of traveling there one day.

9. I'd rather not talk about a(n) .... subject like politics at the dinner table!

10. There was such .... in his answer that I knew nothing more than I did before I asked.

11. Look! There's dried food on this plate; you are not .... enough when you wash the dishes!

12. It can sometimes be difficult to make a(n) .... between a brave decision and a foolish one.

UNIT 5 (A Place to Call Home)

Lead In

A.

- What do you like/dislike about the building that you live in?
- Where would you choose to live if money was not an issue?
- Do you think that the area you live in has a good community spirit?

B. Use the correct form of the words in the box to complete the sentences.
All the words are connected to the theme of housing. Use each word once only.

decor	household	penthouse	mortgage	
real estate agent	slum	double-glazing	surveyor	
exchange	evict	squatter	renovate	tenant
neighbourhood	landlord	lease	destitute	mansion

1. Our .... has decided to put the rent up again.

2. We need .... in these windows to keep out the noise from the traffic.

3. Once you have .... contracts with the seller, you are legally responsible for insuring the property.

4. The .... man had no idea where he would sleep that night or if he would have anything to eat.

5. In order to buy the house we needed to take out a .... from the bank.

6. This is a very safe ....; there is hardly any crime here.

7. I like this apartment but I think I would change the .... as the walls are too pink for my taste.

8. It must be a very wealthy person who lives in that huge ....

9. We've got a great view from our .... apartment because it is on the top floor.

10. The .... have to pay the rent every month.

11. Before buying the house, you need to get a .... to check there are no structural problems.

12. We have a .... on this property for a year.

13. Once the old house has been .... we will be able to move into it.

14. The students were .... from the house because they didn't pay the rent.

15. We try to keep a happy .... here although we do have the odd argument.

16. You'll end up living in a .... if you take drugs and lose your job.

17. The .... showed us several houses before we found one that we liked.

18. .... moved in to the empty house last year and they have been living there ever since.

Reading - 1

Pre-reading - Group work
A.

How important is it to you to own your own home?

Do you believe that buying property is a good way to invest your money?

How easy is it to get a mortgage in your country?

First Reading

B. Read the text and say if the statements are true or false. Correct the false statements.

1. Peer pressure causes people to commit to more than they can really afford to buy.

2. It is better to hold on to a property that is losing value than to sell it quickly.

3. Chuck Brady's friends deserted him when he bought a house in Connecticut.

4. The main reason people choose to live in an area is that it has good schools.

5. When prices become very high in a city like New York, they tend to suddenly crash.

6. In some areas it is sometimes better to rent a property than to buy.

The Ins and Outs of Real Estate in America

1 Confused about the direction of the housing market? It's no wonder. You hear stories about sellers slashing listing prices to attract buyers, but home prices nationally have risen more than 10% over the past year. Inventories of unsold homes are on the rise, yet James Markson, director of homebuilder Lennar Corporation, just reported a 34% jump in company earnings and the much-feared rise in 30-year mortgage rates has failed to materialise.

2 It can be hard to know what to do in this **muddled** situation, whether you're on the buyer's end of the seesaw or the seller's. Cut your price now or hold out for more? Rent or buy? Go for a bigger house or a smaller one? Let's be honest: no one can predict with certainty which way home prices will go in the next year or so. Over the past several years almost everyone who has tried to forecast the direction of the housing market has been wrong. We can, however, tell you how to avoid some critical psychological and financial mistakes in today's anxious markets. No matter how **smart** you are, it's easy to fall into certain mental traps that can cost big bucks. Instead of concentrating on the **fundamentals**, people tend to be ruled by their feelings and the **compulsion** to compare themselves with their neighbours; if my brother-in-law **has made a killing in** real estate, surely I can do the same.

3 A first rule of thumb is to avoid herd behaviour, which is what lured a lot of people into overpriced housing in the first place. The expectation of rising prices became a self-fulfilling prophecy as office mates and in-laws tried to leap-frog each other. The **prevailing** mindset according to James Duckworth of the Consumer Research Institute was: "You see people who aren't particularly talented, who aren't hard-working, who buy a house with nothing down, and they've been getting rich doing it". Another attraction of herd behaviour is the perception of safety in numbers. Millions of buyers can't be wrong, can they?

4 In a softening real estate market, one of the most dangerous mental mistakes is what behavioural economists like Tina Brady call "loss aversion," which is the tendency to do **dumb** things to avoid, at all costs, recording a loss. Some sellers are so averse, they gamble the market will bounce back rather than cut their prices. Indeed, real estate agents often have a much clearer idea than sellers that demand has softened.

5 Even owners who stand to make a big profit on a sale often set the price too high. In this case the mental error isn't loss aversion but outdated thinking. New research shows that sellers set their listing price, in part, based on information six months to nine months old. That means if you don't pay close attention, you will tend to underprice in a rising market and overprice in a falling one. The **gravest** danger of **dragging your heels** on price cuts in a sinking market is that you can "follow the market down," never managing to sell because your price is always a little bit too high.

6 In upscale communities, social pressure to buy is intense. Chuck Brady, managing director of Brady Technology, recalls that when he and his family moved to **upper-crust** Darien, Connecticut, fifteen years ago and rented for a year, "we were absolutely second-class citizens. It was very unpleasant." Call it "castle thinking" - the notion that a home is a fortress against a cruel world and it's perfectly defensible.

7 But in many markets the total monthly costs of renting are far below the total monthly costs of owning the same property - 62% cheaper in San Diego, for example. So you owe it to yourself to be aware that your castle thinking can be a costly predilection.

8 What people can do is be aware of their human tendency towards status seeking. Learn to channel your drive more productively. If getting your kids into a good school district is a priority, for example, try to satisfy your lust for status by buying a small-ish house in a **prime** school district instead of a showplace in a worse one.

9 Within the U.S. prices in some housing markets do raise red warning flags. A good starting point is to look at the affordability of homes for ordinary families. Of course, unaffordability is a **chronic** condition in cities like New York, so it's not necessarily evidence that a sharp price correction is on the cards. Yet another way to identify a problem area is to compare rents to sales prices. The idea is that if people's monthly payments are much higher than what they would spend to rent the same place, then they must be banking on prices going up so they can sell for a profit someday. That leaves them exposed if prices don't rise.

10 This year millions of American families will buy a home. The process will always be lengthy and, inevitably for those involved, a big deal. But whether you are a buyer or a seller, you just need to be realistic, practical and up-to-date with current market trends.

Second Reading

C. Using your own words as far as possible, answer the questions by reading and interpreting the meaning of the text.

1. In paragraph 1, what negative thing was expected to happen that didn't?

2. In paragraph 4, what does the writer mean by loss aversion?

3. In paragraph 5, what is said can happen if you aren't up-to-date with the housing market?

4. In paragraph 6, what tends to be a negative factor when people are house-hunting?

5. In paragraph 9, what could happen if someone pays a mortgage that is much higher than local rents?

Vocabulary in context

D. Find a word or expression in bold in the text that has the same or a similar meaning to each of the following meanings.

1. silly, foolish _____

2. a strong desire or need to do or have something _____

3. clever _____

4. delay doing something, especially making a decision _____

5. generally held, believed or accepted _____

6. being the most important _____

7. belonging to the highest social class _____

8. the main, basic parts of something _____

9. most serious _____

10. confusing, disorganised _____

11. something that lasts a long time (or is always that way) _____

12. earn a lot of money _____

E. Use the correct form of the words below to complete the sentences. All the words have been taken from the text.

stall	leapfrog	channel	rule
hold out	stand	slash	lure

1. During the sales the shops often .... their prices.

2. Try not to be totally .... by fear; sometimes it's necessary to take a risk!

3. You .... to get a promotion if you continue to work this hard.

4. We need to encourage him to .... his energy into something productive.

5. The signs outside the casino .... him in to have a gamble.

6. Young people today try to .... each other with new technology as they always want the best and most expensive products.

7. If you can .... for a few more days, I will be able to come with you.

8. Try to .... him for a few minutes while I get ready to go.

Exam Strategy

Matching

In this task type, candidates are given a number of options, for example, names of people, and are required to match these options with, for example, a theory, discovery or statement credited to them.* It is possible that some options may go unused, and that others may be used more than once. The instructions will inform candidates if an option may be used more than once.

This task type is often used with discursive texts where current opinions on a topical subject are expressed.

* (see page 71- B)

Your ability to recognise and understand opinions and theories is being tested. An initial skim will help you to understand the gist of the passage. Scanning will be useful to identify where and by whom opinions and theories are expressed – start with the easy thing to locate like a person's name. Careful reading of selected parts of the text may then be required if you're still unsure.

Questions 1 – 3
Look at the following list of statements (Questions 1-3) taken from the passage *The Ins and Outs of Real Estate in America*. Match each statement with the correct person A-D. There is one person too many who should not be used. Write the correct letters A-D for your answers.

1: Reported a significant spike in company earnings of more than one-third.

2: People tend to act rashly in an effort to avoid making a loss in a softening housing market.

3: The experience of renting was an entirely disagreeable one.

| A: Tina Brady | B: James Duckworth | C: Chuck Brady | D: James Markson |

Notes/Table/Summary/Flow-chart Completion:
With this task type, candidates are given some type of summary of a section of the passage, and are required to complete it with information drawn from the passage. Note that the summary will usually be of only one part of the passage rather than the whole.

The summary may be in the form of:
- a text
- a table *(see page 71- C)*
- unconnected notes
- a series of boxes or steps linked by arrows to show a sequence of events *(see page 60 - E)*

The answers aren't necessarily in order, though they usually come from the same section of the text.

Candidates will either have to select words from the passage or select words from a list of answers.
Remember, don't select more than the required number of words from the passage or you'll lose marks.

Complete the summary of paragraph 4 above with words (A-K) from the box.

A: making	D: double-pricing	G: think	J: gamble
B: averse	E: deflated	H: high	K: lottery
C: pray	F: low	I: overpricing	

In a softening retail market, people tend to become loss (4) _____. Some sellers would rather (5) _____ that the market will bounce back than cut their prices. Real estate agents usually see the signs of a softening market before sellers. Indeed, sellers often list their prices based on outdated information, which means there can be under-pricing in a rising market and (6) _____ in a falling one. Sellers who continue to use outdated information in a softening market are in danger of following the market down as their prices are always too (7) _____.

Questions 8 – 10
Complete the summary of paragraph 2 below.
Choose NO MORE THAN TWO WORDS from the passage for each answer.

The situation is quite confusing, so whether you're on the buyer's end of (8) _____ or the seller's, the question is what you should do. Is it best to cut your (9) _____ or hold out for more? Rent or buy? Upgrade or down-grade? It is difficult to predict which way house prices will go, although many people have attempted to do this. We should, though, learn to avoid some (10) _____ psychological and financial mistakes in today's nervous market. It is vital that people be aware of the mental traps they can fall into and put aside personal feelings and the compulsion to make comparisons with their neighbours if they are to survive in these turbulent times.

Questions 11-13
Complete the summary of paragraphs 8 and 9 below.
Choose NO MORE THAN THREE WORDS from the passage for each answer.

People must be wary of (11) _____ towards seeking status. They should live within their means and make wise decisions. Why not buy a small house in a prime location if the priority is getting your kids into a good school, rather than a showpiece in an area with an undesirable school. Prices in some housing markets do raise (12) _____. If homes aren't affordable (13) _____ then this might be a sign that a sharp price correction is on the cards.

Vocabulary

A. Study the text to try to understand the meaning of the words in bold.

NYC Hotline set up to deal with difficult neighbours

A new hotline has been launched in New York which will allow residents to report their **unruly** neighbours to the authorities. The hotline will be advertised on posters and leaflets and is part of a $90 million programme to **combat** antisocial behaviour in New York's streets. Residents will be able to use the number to report problems such as graffiti, **abandoned** vehicles and rowdy behaviour.

The scheme which is being described as "ASBO hotline" - with reference to antisocial behaviour orders - has one national number. Callers are then **put through** to their local office after providing their zip code. Each complaint will be dealt with by a local **body** - consisting of the police, local authorities and other agencies - which acts under guidance from the government's antisocial behaviour unit. A government spokesman said that as soon as a complaint is made it is forwarded to the relevant agency to be dealt with. However, residents will be told to refer more serious problems straight to the police.

The scheme has already been **piloted** in some parts of the city and it is to be extended to the entire area by the end of this month. While the government is **heralding** the move as a significant step toward **tackling** 'nuisance neighbours', critics say it is nothing more than a **gimmick** by the government to win votes. One critic said: "People in this country need more police on the streets, not these hotlines. You won't get rid of antisocial behaviour by setting up a hotline. What we need is a criminal system that punishes, rather than gimmicks like this and new proposals month after month."

The hotline is the latest move in the Together Campaign which was launched by the government as the umbrella movement for a series of **initiatives**. The project identified begging as a form of antisocial behaviour and made it a recordable offence. As a result, the number of beggars in those areas within the project's scope has been significantly reduced. A government spokesperson said: "We have brought in tough new laws and an ambitious action plan, providing the tools and the expertise for police and local agencies to tackle the troublesome minority who can **blight** communities and make people's lives hell." However, critics of the scheme say that headline-grabbing initiatives are not being **backed** with enough action and that the government needs to concentrate on enforcement rather than gimmick schemes which promise much but, in reality, do little

B. Complete these sentences with the correct form of one of the words or phrases in bold in the text.

1. The athlete is .... by an international company that is sponsoring her.

2. A new parking scheme has been .... this year to try to make the city centre more pedestrian-friendly.

3. The teacher shouted at the .... children and told them to be quiet and sit down.

4. We need to .... this problem quickly before it gets any worse.

5. You can only be .... to the director's office if you phone the reception first.

6. The police are determined to .... drug dealing in this area.

7. The government has launched a new .... to improve schools in poorer areas.

8. The bad behaviour of a few people .... the day for everyone else.

9. The new drug has been .... as a major advance in the treatment of cancer.

10. It's not a particularly useful product; it's more a .... to publicise the company.

11. From the pile of .... books on the floor, I worked out that the children had not finished their work.

12. Several local .... have raised money for the new park.

Homophones

C. A homophone is a word that sounds the same as another word but has a different meaning and spelling. Look at the pairs of homophones below. You have been given synonyms or definitions for each word. Try to work out what the words are. There is an example at the beginning.

guilt	pain	key	due	soul	gilt	air	chord	heir	sole
pore	dew	pane	scent	quay	pair	cord	cent	pour	pear

eg. a) receive money for work done   <u>earn</u>
  b) container like a vase with two handles   <u>urn</u>

1. a) something used to open a lock   ....

  b) the edge of a port or harbour   ....

2. a) something owed, especially money   ....

  b) drops of water that form on plants or grass ....

3. a) a bad feeling you have if you have done something wrong ....

  b) covering of gold   ....

4. a) what we breathe   ....

  b) person who will inherit something   ....

5. a) the bottom of a foot or shoe   ....

  b) the non-physical part of a person   ....

6. a) a physical feeling when you are hurt   ....

  b) a piece of glass for a window   ....

7. a) perfume   ....

  b) American coin   ....

8. a) two of something   ....

  b) a kind of fruit   ....

9. a) a piece of rope or string   ....

  b) a number of musical notes played at the same time ....

10. a) put a liquid over something   ....

  b) small opening found all over the skin   ....

D. Choose a word from exercise C to complete the sentences below.

1. I could smell the .... that she had been wearing even after she'd left the room.

2. Who is going to pay for a new .... of glass to put in the broken window?

3. Shall I .... some fresh cream over the fruit?

4. Don't sit on the grass, it's covered with .... and you'll get wet.

5. There's a hole in the .... of one of my shoes.

6. He is the .... to a large estate so he will be rich when his father dies.

7. It was so hot that I seemed to be sweating from every single .... of my skin.

8. I chose a beautiful .... frame for the picture.

E. Complete the flow-chart using options A-G. The are two options that you will not need to use.

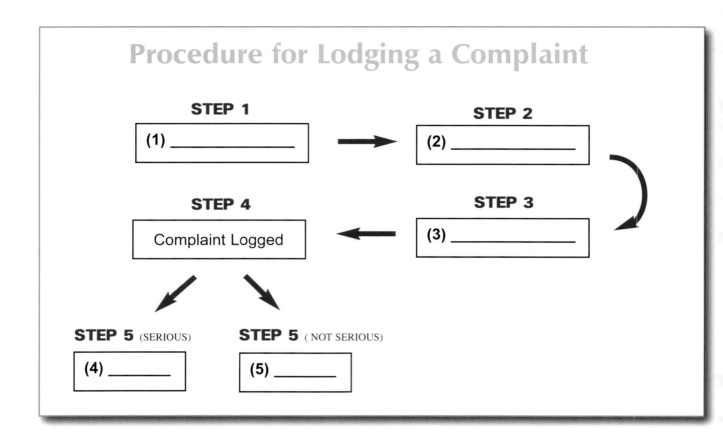

Procedure for Lodging a Complaint

STEP 1
(1) _____

STEP 2
(2) _____

STEP 3
(3) _____

STEP 4
Complaint Logged

STEP 5 (SERIOUS)
(4) _____

STEP 5 (NOT SERIOUS)
(5) _____

(A) Provide Zip Code
(B) Complaint brought to attention of relevant agency
(C) Call hotline number
(D) Complainant directed to contact Police
(E) Call redirected to local office
(F) Complaint resolved
(G) Complainant called back

F.

Part 1

Decide whether the following statements are True (T) or False (F), or write Not Given (NG) if the information is not in the text.

1. The new hotline is part of a project which aims to tackle antisocial behaviour. _____
2. Callers to the hotline are transferred to their local office before having to supply any information over the phone. _____
3. The scheme was tested in certain areas of the city and is now being rolled out more widely. _____
4. This is the first time the government has launched a series of schemes under one main umbrella campaign. _____
5. Some people are sceptical of the government's agenda and do not believe the schemes are being supported by sufficient action by the government. _____

Part 2

Within the five statements written above, you will find a synonym (or word/phrase of similar meaning) for each of the following words/phrases from the original text. Write down the synonym in the space provided.

(A) PILOTED   _____
(B) PUT THROUGH   _____
(C) COMBAT   _____
(D) BACKED WITH   _____
(E) INITIATIVES   _____

Reading - 2

Pre-Reading

A. Think about the questions below. Write short answers and then read the text.

1. How many different kinds of houses can you think of? (In answering this question, try to think about cultures other than your own.)

2. 'A nomadic lifestyle is one where people always move from place to place never settling down'. What are the advantages and disadvantages of this kind of lifestyle?

3. What do you think would be the hardest place in the world to live in, in terms of comfort and quality of life?

Ice Houses

The construction principles of the igloo are **ingenious**. It is not just a highly functional habitation but also a perfect expression of the adaptation of function and form to fit the arctic environment.

The igloo utilises what must be one of the weakest of building materials - frozen water - and its structure gives this unlikely material great strength. Its form is not only beautiful, but also a shape that is surprisingly strong. The igloo is not a perfect hemispherical dome but more of an egg shape - technically speaking, a catenary arch - about the strongest form in nature. A correctly-built igloo will support the weight of a man standing on its roof.

Frozen water - snow and ice - also has other striking **qualities**. It's the only readily available building material in much of the Arctic and is, of course, a completely renewable resource. Ice is a construction material that causes no pollution whatsoever in its manufacture, use or disposal. This **paradoxical** material is also an incomparable insulator, so that an igloo keeps out external cold while retaining all the internal heat that is generated. Consequently, an igloo can resist the onslaught of the fiercest freezing gale, while its interior remains warm. On the outside, temperatures may be as low as −45 °C, but on the inside they may range from −7 °C to 6 °C when warmed by body heat alone. By the simple act of lining the living area with animal skin, the temperature within may be increased to up to 20 °C

When an igloo is built, the particular kind of wind-compacted snow needed for construction is located, then blocks are cut, traditionally using an ivory knife. The first three rows of blocks are laid, one upon the other, with sides nearly vertical. Then halfway through the fourth row, a wedge-shape block is cut that enables the sides to be constructed in a continuous **spiral** - a far stronger construction technique than stacking row upon row. This is the key that allows the dome to be self-supporting during construction. The blocks are held firmly in place by friction and freezing; surfaces to be joined are rubbed with the ice saw to melt the ice with the heat of friction and the blocks are held together until they freeze, with the ice acting as **mortar**. Sometimes blocks of clear ice are included to form a window, placed carefully to admit as much scarce winter light as possible.

But perhaps the most remarkable aspect of igloo construction is the lamp **seasoning** that takes place after it is built. After the last snow block has been inserted, the igloo is tightly **sealed** and a lamp is lit inside. The heated air, having no exit, begins to melt the internal face of the snow blocks, which rapidly freeze again when cold air is again admitted from the outside. In this way each snow block is firmly cemented in place and converted to ice on its inner face. Occupation for a few days then gradually changes the composition of all of the blocks, so that the structure is no longer a snow house but a house of solid ice. This transformation is responsible for the igloo's remarkable stability; and so solid is it that half the igloo may be destroyed without compromising the remaining structure.

The internal structure of an igloo is no less ingenious. Hot air rises while cold air sinks, so cold **settles** in the lower portion of the interior and the warm air rises into the dome where it is trapped. Following this same principle, the sleeping area consists of a raised platform and a sunken entrance area, a tunnel built below ground level and often so low that people must go on their hands and knees to pass through, acts as a cold trap, preventing icy external air from being admitted to the main chamber as the **occupants** enter. A saucer shaped stone that acts as a lamp is placed several feet above the floor, filled with burning seal-oil, and a stone cooking pot suspended above it.

Unfortunately, igloo construction is a dying art. This is partly to do with changing culture - younger Inuits prefer to live in timber houses flown in from Denmark, and have little interest in learning the mystery of igloo construction. But perhaps more alarmingly, the **demise** of the igloo has to do with climate change. The area within the Arctic circle is now one of the most rapidly warming places on the planet. Here temperatures are rising nearly twice as fast as for the rest of the Earth and the permanent sea-ice cover has declined by almost 40% in the past 30 years. This means that building igloos in the areas where the Inuits live and hunt is becoming increasingly difficult. Snow of the right **consistency** is harder to find and it is ever more difficult to freeze blocks together. This perfectly adapted **dwelling** is no longer perfectly adapted to its changing environment.

First Reading

A. Do the following statements reflect the views of the writer in the reading passage? Write YES if the statement reflects the views of the writer, NO if the statement contradicts the views of the writer, and NOT GIVEN if it is impossible to say what the writer thinks about this.

1. The igloo was traditionally well-suited to its environment
2. Igloos are attractive to look at.
3. Igloos are shaped like a hemispherical dome.
4. Snow is an environmentally friendly building material.
5. Most Europeans would feel cold in an igloo.
6. Igloos are not easy to build.
7. The entire igloo is built in a spiral.
8. It's dark in the winter in the arctic.
9. The occupants take care not to melt the igloo.
10. It's not important to continue building igloos.
11. In 30 years there will be no more sea ice.

1.	
2.	
3.	
4.	
5.	
6.	
7.	
8.	
9.	
10.	
11.	

Second Reading

C. Label the diagram using NO MORE THAN THREE WORDS from the original text for each answer.

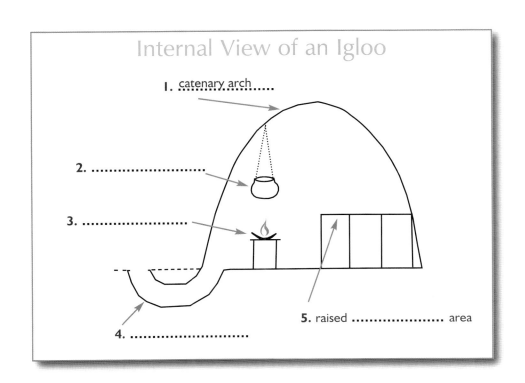

Internal View of an Igloo

1. catenary arch
2. ....
3. ....
4. ....
5. raised .... area

Vocabulary in context

D. Find a word or expression in bold in the text that has the same meaning as (or a similar meaning to) each of the following

1. a shape that winds around, with each curve above or outside of the previous one
2. particular characteristics of a person or thing
3. the people who live or work in a place
4. texture of a substance; how thick or smooth it is
5. slowly sinks down and becomes still
6. clever; involving new ideas or methods
7. a place where someone lives
8. something with contradictory qualities or characteristics
9. tightly closed; nothing can enter or escape
10. the end or death of something
11. a process of slowly allowing something to become ready for some use
12. a mixture of sand, water and cement used to hold bricks together

1.	
2.	
3.	
4.	
5.	
6.	
7.	
8.	
9.	
10.	
11.	
12.	

E. Use the correct form of the words from Exercise D above to complete the sentences.

1. In a few minutes the tea leaves will .... to the bottom of the cup.

2. You must allow the wood to .... before you can build with it.

3. Jenny has many good ....

4. If you don't .... the bottle carefully, it might spill in your bag.

5. I never saw the .... of the old mansion on the end of my street.

6. She's a ....child; trying to be the centre of attention one moment, then painfully shy the next.

7. I don't mind the taste of eggs, but I don't like their .... at all.

8. The sea shell formed a beautiful ....

9. Small plants were growing between the bricks where the .... had fallen out.

10. It was only because of Jose's .... idea to park the car and continue by metro that we arrived on time.

11. That cave is probably the .... of some wild animal.

12. No one knows the reason for the .... of the dinosaurs.

UNIT 6 [Education for All]

Lead In

A.

- They say that your schooldays are the best days of your life. To what extent would you agree with this statement?
- Have you ever been bullied or witnessed anyone else being bullied?
- If a child witnesses another child being bullied, what should he or she do?

B. Use the correct form of the words in the box to complete the sentences. All the words are connected to the theme of education. Use each word once only.

coach	tutor	demonstrate	enlighten	drill
dissertation	faculty	term	apprentice	bookworm
novice	prodigy	authority	discipline	proficient
campus	edit	unschooled		

1. Billy's such a(n) .... ; he never stops reading.

2. I have to write a 10,000 word .... as part of my degree.

3. You need to .... your work before you hand it in to make sure that there are no mistakes.

4. Let me .... how to do it and then you can all have a go after.

5. The academic year is divided into three ....

6. One way of teaching is to .... students so that they repeat what the teacher has said.

7. Doctor Jones is a leading .... on this subject.

8. If you don't know how I managed to do that, let me .... you.

9. My tennis .... teaches me twice a week.

10. If you are struggling to understand the work, you should consider hiring a private .... to teach you.

11. Smoking is not allowed anywhere on the university ....

12. Alison teaches in the .... of Fine Arts.

13. I'm only a(n) .... at this so you can't expect me to do it perfectly.

14. The teacher .... the naughty children.

15. I have managed to get a position as a(n) .... to an electrician.

16. Not until you are .... as a driver, will you be able to pass the test.

17. I don't see how he can comment on the subject when he is completely .... in it.

18. George is a bit of a maths .... ; he already knows more than most children twice his age.

Reading - 1

Pre-reading

A. Tell the class about a teacher that made a strong impression on you, either in a positive or negative way. What qualities do you think make a good teacher?

In fine voice - the stress of teaching

Confidence, presentation and communication skills are recognised weapons in most teachers' **armouries**, but few would consider the voice to be their most prized asset. The teacher's voice is in constant use, but unlike other professional voice users, such as actors and singers, many receive little training in how to look after it. If Pavarotti has a sore throat, he can cancel the show. Teachers are expected to struggle on, accepting husky voices as an occupational hazard. But putting the voice under continual strain can lead to long-lasting damage.

At Harvard University School of Education, voice training for student teachers is a priority. "Teaching is about communication, and the voice is the main tool of communication," says James Williams, teacher training convenor in the School of Education. "Not training teachers about voice skills would be like training a surgeon to do an operation without explaining the tools or instruments to use."

Trainees at Harvard are given two sessions on voice and self-presentation run by the voice specialist Julie Stanford, during their **induction** period in the first two weeks of the course. School mentors are made aware of the voice training and asked to refer student teachers who need help with voice and self-presentation to Stanford. Trainees who would like further help with their voice can attend a series of voluntary workshops on voice care.

"Teachers are very bad at seeing themselves as professional voice users," says Stanford, "so we make it clear to the students from the **outset**. The message is very simple: if there's no voice, there's no job." During training, students learn about the anatomy of the voice and voice care. There is also **input** on pitch, pace and effective intonation in the classroom context. Accent is another key topic - not the **elimination** of accent, but how students can communicate clearly in the classroom without accent or dialect getting in the way. Student teachers are asked to prepare a three-minute individual presentation for their **peers**, which is filmed, pro-

viding opportunities for self-evaluation. Students also receive **feedback** from Stanford. An increasing number of teacher training providers are recognising the need to offer voice training, but for more experienced teachers, bad habits may already be **ingrained**. According to Jack Denning, coordinator of the Voice Care Network, a charitable organisation that provides support and information for teachers, many lack knowledge about how to protect their most valuable asset. "The muscles in the voice are affected by stress and emotion," says Denning. "Teaching is a very stressful job, so you can imagine the impact on the voice. Unfortunately, lack of knowledge about voice care means that many teachers **abuse** their voices without even realising it."

Bad habits include throat clearing, which pushes the vocal chords together; failure to drink enough water; talking too quickly, which can affect breathing; and speaking in too high or deep a pitch. Trainee teachers are made aware of the signs of vocal stress and how to avoid it. A **persistent** tickly cough, hoarse throat, **tenderness** or a noticeable change in vocal quality are all danger signs that shouldn't be ignored. And Denning believes teachers can avoid vocal stress by making use of non-verbal signals to attract students' attention.

Environmental factors also have a part to play. "I have often wondered how much thought goes into the acoustic design of classrooms when **refurbishments** are carried out or new schools are built." says Denning. "It is a key factor when building a theatre. It should also be a key factor when designing a school."

First Reading

B. Read the text and say if the statements are True or False. Correct the false statements.

. Trainee teachers are given singing classes to make their voice stronger.

....

. Trainee teachers at Harvard observe experienced teachers to discuss how they use their voice.

....

. It doesn't matter where a teacher comes from as long as their voice is clear.

....

. People who have been teaching for a long time usually know how to protect their voice.

....

. Dehydration is a common cause of voice strain.

....

. Denning specialises in designing classrooms.

....

Second Reading

C. Using your own words as far as possible, answer the questions by reading and interpreting the meaning of the text.

. In paragraph one, what does the writer mean by describing teachers' voices as 'their most prized asset'?

_____

_____

. In paragraph two, why does James Williams refer to the training of surgeons?

_____

_____

. When are trainee teachers first made aware of how they appear to others?

_____

_____

. Why is it difficult for experienced teachers to change their habits?

_____

_____

. What can be done to reduce the amount of time a teacher spends talking?

_____

_____

Vocabulary in context

D. Find a word or expression in bold in the text that has the same meaning as (or a similar meaning to) each of the following

1. start, beginning _____

2. continuing for a long time or happening frequently _____

3. be very much a part of something or of the way someone behaves or thinks _____

4. a collection of things for some purpose; original meaning is a collection of weapons _____

5. people of the same age, class and status as yourself _____

6. a procedure for introducing someone to a new job, organisation or way of life _____

7. the act of changing and improving or modernising a place _____

8. the act of getting rid of something or somebody _____

9. a feeling of slight pain _____

10. to use something in the wrong way; treat cruelly _____

11. comments given in response to something somebody has done _____

12. something added or contributed (action, comments, ideas etc) _____

E. Use the correct form of the words or phrases below to complete the sentences. All the words have been taken from the text.

series	key	asset	impact
struggle	hazard	mentor	pace

1. He .... to keep running when he was close to the end of the marathon.

2. The .... issue here is whether he will agree to help us or not.

3. The bad weather has had a negative .... on tourism this year.

4. Mrs Smith was my .... when I was doing the teacher training course.

5. One of the .... of this sport is that it is very easy to injure yourself.

6. One of his greatest .... is his willingness to try new things.

7. It is better to walk at a slower .... for a long time than to run for only ten minutes.

8. It was a whole .... of incidents that led to the current situation.

Exam Strategy

Read this article for gist first, to get an overall understanding.
Refer back to the notes in Unit 5 on matching tasks. A useful tip is to scan the passage for names A-C and/or key words in statements 1-7, then read the relevant sections of the passage carefully.

Questions 1 – 7

Look at the following list of statements (Questions 1-7) taken from the passage above *(page 86)*.

Match each statement with the correct person A - C. More than one statement may be matched with each person.

Write the correct letter A, B or C for your answer.

A: Julie Stanford	B: Jack Denning	C: James Williams

ANSWER

1:   Teaches trainees about voice and self-presentation at Harvard university.   _____

2:   Believes the voice is the main tool of communication.   _____

3:   Thinks that many teachers harm their voice without realising it.   _____

4:   Believes that a teacher who cannot speak cannot work.   _____

5:   Believes teachers usually don't consider themselves professional voice users.   _____

6:   He/she has the opinion that acoustics should be a key factor to consider when designing schools.   _____

7:   Thinks that it is absolutely necessary for teachers to be trained in how to use their voice.   _____

You may wish to refer back to the notes on Sentence Completion in Unit 4 before doing the tasks below. Remember that it is wise to scan the article in order to quickly locate the sentences.

Questions 8 – 11
Complete the sentences below.
Choose NO MORE THAN TWO WORDS from the passage for each answer.

Write your answers below.

8:    Putting the voice under _____ can cause long-lasting damage.

9:    Harvard University School of Education regards the provision of voice training as _____ .

10:   During training there is input on _____ and effective intonation in the classroom context.

11:   An increasing number of teacher training providers _____ the need to offer voice training.

Questions 12-14
Complete each sentence with the correct ending A-F from the box below.
Write the correct letter A-F on the answer line.

A very powerful and resilient.	**D** danger sign that shouldn't be ignored.
B annoys students as it's hard to understand.	**E** common complaint of teachers.
C affected by stress and emotion.	**F** can affect breathing.

12:   The muscles in the voice are   _____

13:   Talking too quickly   _____

14:   A persistent tickly cough is a   _____

Vocabulary

Vocabulary

. Study the text to try to understand the meaning of the words in bold.

Beating the playground Blues

For most young pupils, playground spats and scuffles are all part of growing up. But at one school, potentially **explosive** situations are **defused** by patrols of a select group of children, sometimes as young as six, wearing badges and red caps bearing the word 'mentor'. They are trained in 'anger management and conflict resolution' and, under the 'peer mediation scheme', they also stop bullying among the pupils - who include children as young as three.

The scheme at St Ann's school - the **brainchild** of headteacher Samantha Murray - is being introduced to another six schools in the same area, after its success there.

"I'd hate people to think this is a namby-pamby scheme and that we don't believe in **reprimanding** our students," she said yesterday. "But this has a far longer-lasting effect on children." The mentors help children to walk away from arguments and fights while breathing techniques are also used to deal with anger. Mrs Murray said "as soon as children get really cross with each other, the mentor appears and says, 'Would you like to talk about it?' " Children listen better to their friends than teachers sometimes.

The 22 mentors are chosen by staff each year from volunteers aged six to eleven. They meet once a week for an hour-long session about anger management, conflict resolution and problem-solving. The youngsters are shown how to **mediate** and they act out scenarios which might need their involvement. One technique is called SARAH and teaches pupils how to deal with angry pupils. It consists of five steps: Stop talking; Activate listening; Repeat back what is said to you; Accept feelings of others; and Help others to make choices.

At break times, the mentors are **on hand** to break up or stop fights and **console** bullied children. Unhappy or angry pupils can go to the Friendship Stop - a bench in the playground where mentors give advice or counselling. There is also a Peace Patrol of a dozen pupils who wear green caps and act as prefects to keep order. "This is a violent area and children are used to witnessing quite a lot of violence," said Mrs Murray. 'We were concerned that sometimes this **spilled into** the playground. The school is also in a **deprived** area. A lot of the children don't have good role models at home. Fighting was a problem for all age groups so we wanted a bottom-up approach for children to take control of their own anger management. It's about giving them opportunities and techniques to become part of a group and make friends.'

The headteacher, who has a diploma in **pastoral** care and counselling in schools, added: 'Since we introduced the scheme three years ago, discipline at the school has really improved. I have not had to **split up** a fight for ages. Before there were two or three a week. The school has a nice atmosphere because the children are happy and pleasant. We do follow other disciplinary methods as well but there has to be an **element** of children taking charge of themselves.'

The scheme's expansion is being funded by a $40,000 grant from the *Children's Fund* and *New Deal for Communities*.

B. Complete these sentences with the correct form of one of the words or phrases in bold in the text.

1. I couldn't .... her when her father died because she was grieving so much.

2. Don't worry, I'll be .... if you need me to help with anything.

3. This organisation .... between employers and employees when there is a dispute.

4. He tried to .... the situation by telling a joke when it became tense between them.

5. It is believed that children who grow up in a(n) .... area are more likely to turn to crime.

6. The teacher .... the two boys who were hitting each other.

7. The girls were severely .... for stealing the candy.

8. There must be a(n) .... of truth in what he is saying.

9. That great idea was the .... of the managing director.

10. The argument was sure to .... the playground when the lesson was finished.

11. You had better be careful with what you say in such a(n) .... situation.

12. Your personal tutor is responsible for your .... care as well as your studies.

Word Building

C. Complete the sentences by using a derivative of the word given in parenthesis and adding a suitable adverb-particle from the box below.

out	down	in	by	up	on	under

1. There has been a terrible .... of the disease in the south of the country.   (BREAK)

2. What made him .... such a difficult task?   (TAKE)

3. The police told the .... to move away from the scene of the accident.   (LOOK)

4. The emergency services will be on .... in case the stunt goes wrong.   (STAND)

5. We got absolutely soaked in the .... because we didn't have an umbrella.   (POUR)

6. There's been a(n) .... at the bank and one man has been shot.   (HOLD)

7. Your sugar .... is far too high.   (TAKE)

8. She had a nervous .... after her husband died.   (BREAK)

9. Taking drugs is sure to be his .... in the end.   (FALL)

10. He gave a(n) .... speech to encourage the students before their exams.   (LIFT)

11. She had to .... a long operation on her badly injured leg.   (GO)

12. She will die of the .... disease.   (CURE)

The Irish Education System

In Ireland, it is not compulsory for children to take part in pre-primary education. Nonetheless, many parents choose to send their children to private institutes for this purpose at around the age of three or four. The state, however, does not stipulate exactly what children should be taught in these schools, nor is there any particular official state-sanctioned body which oversees what goes on in them.

All children must enrol in primary level education though. Most do so from about the age of four or five, and once children reach six years of age, the state obliges parents to enrol them if they haven't already been enrolled. In Ireland, it is compulsory to remain in education until you are sixteen; effective therefore, every single young person must go through the primary school system. Primary school is made up of eight separate grades; junior and senior infants, and first to sixth class.

Once a student has finished sixth class, he then transfers into a secondary school. Secondary school is comprised of the Junior Cycle (after completion of which students sit their first major exam - the Junior Certificate), Transition Year, and the Senior Cycle. Transition year is a relatively new programme introduced by the department of education. It allows students to have a 'light' year, academically speaking, between the exam-oriented Junior and Senior cycles. During Transition Year, emphasis is put on extra-curricular activities and students are given the chance to learn new skills. Despite its popularity with both stu-

dents and teachers, Transition Year remains optional; some schools choose to run the programme and others bypass it moving straight into the Senior Cycle instead. The Senior Cycle is extremely important for students because they sit their final school exam at the end of it; this is known as the Leaving Certificate. A student's performance in this exam will determine whether or not they will get accepted into university to study the course of their choice. Students can study as many subjects as they want during the two years of the Senior Cycle; however, only six will count towards their aggregate points score in the assessment system for college entry. Students rarely study more than seven subjects given the challenging nature of the curriculum.

School-leavers, typically aged between 17 and 19, must then decide whether or not to go into third-level study. For those who decide they wish to, and who are lucky enough to fulfill the entry requirements of their chosen course, higher education is, ostensibly, free. That said, in reality, the registration fees charged by universities and colleges today are so expensive that students are effectively paying college entrance fees, just by another name. Unlike in the other levels of the education system (where the option to enrol in a school is determined by its proximity to where you live) students may study in the location of their choice, whether it be near or far away.

A. Match each statement, A - L, to the appropriate level within the education system. The first one is done for you as an example.

(A) Attendance is not mandatory though many young children are sent here.

(B) There is no restriction imposed on the location of one's place of study at this level.

(C) This is the only level which is compulsory for everyone to complete.

(D) There is no limit on the number of exam subjects a student may study, but results will only count in a set number of subjects.

(E) Entry into courses at this level is determined on the basis of the results of a final examination at the previous level of stud

(F) The syllabus is not determined by the state or regulated by any official body.

(G) Attendance is mandatory for all children who reach a certain age.

(H) Students effectively pay for their education at this level, despite the fact that it is supposed to be free.

(I) Students spend more years of their education attending school at this level than any other.

(J) There are no state-run or state-sponsored institutions operating at this level.

(K) This level is divided into three different phases, one of which is optional.

(L) Attendance is compulsory, but only up to a certain age.

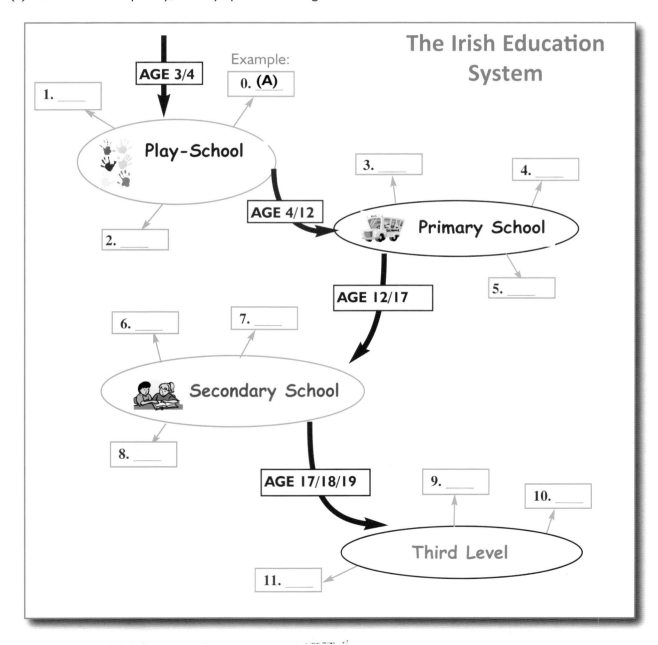

The Irish Education System

AGE 3/4

Example: 0. **(A)**

1. ____

Play-School

2. ____

AGE 4/12

3. ____

4. ____

Primary School

5. ____

AGE 12/17

6. ____

7. ____

Secondary School

8. ____

AGE 17/18/19

9. ____

10. ____

11. ____

Third Level

UNIT 7 [The Earth under threat]

Lead-In

A.

- What kinds of pollution problems exist in the area that you live in?
- What, if anything, do you and your family recycle?
- Is the area that you live in being developed in any way? How?
- What can people do in their home to save energy?

B. Use the words in the box below to complete the sentences. All the words are connected to the theme of the environment.

emissions	smog	slick	drought	resources
famine	poverty	erosion	timber	industrialisation

1. The cutting of .... from forests is a contributing factor to flooding in this area.

2. After months without rain, ... became inevitable.

3. The .... of the area has destroyed many species of flora that used to inhabit the land which is now occupied by factories.

4. Many people are living in .... here because there is no work and very little food.

5. The oil .... has killed thousands of fish and seabirds.

6. The .... in the city was so thick that we could actually see it in the air.

7. Carbon .... from cars are one of the worst pollutants.

8. We are using up the Earth's natural .... faster than they can be replaced.

9. The .... in Africa is so bad that millions of people have died of hunger.

10. Rising seas are causing the .... of coastal cliffs.

Reading - 1

Pre-reading - Group Work

A. Look at the phrases and expressions below and discuss what they mean. Use a dictionary to help you if you need to. Discuss which are relevant to the place where you live and which may have an effect on your neighbourhood in the future.

scorched earth	raging storms	torrential rain
melting icecaps	global warming	greenhouse effect

First Reading

B. Look at the information below and decide if you think the information is likely to be true or false. Then scan the text and see if your predictions were correct. Discuss with other students anything that you find surprising.

1. Global warming is progressing faster than scientists first thought.
_____
_____

2. People will be forced to move to low-lying coastal areas because of climate change.
_____
_____

3. Man-made pollution is the main cause of global warming.
_____
_____

4. The majority of scientists still deny that man is the main cause of the Earth's climate problems despite the panel's findings.
_____
_____

5. It's impossible to stop global warming now.
_____
_____

Global warming: the final verdict

Global warming is destined to have a far more destructive and earlier impact than previously estimated, the most authoritative report yet produced on climate change will warn next week. A draft copy of the Fourth Assessment Report of the Intergovernmental Panel on Climate Change (the IPCC), shows the frequency of devastating storms will increase dramatically. Sea levels will rise over the century by around half a meter; snow will disappear from all but the highest mountains; deserts will spread; oceans will become acidic, leading to the destruction of coral reefs and atolls; and deadly heat waves will become more prevalent. The impact will be catastrophic, forcing hundreds of millions of people to **flee** their devastated homelands, particularly in tropical, low-lying areas, while creating waves of immigrants whose movements will strain the economies of even the most **affluent** countries.

'The really chilling thing about the IPCC report is that it is the work of several thousand climate experts who have widely differing views about how greenhouse gases will affect the planet. Some think they will have a major impact; *others* a lesser role. Each paragraph of this report was therefore argued over and **scrutinised** intensely. Only points that were considered indisputable survived this process. This is a very conservative document - that's what makes it so scary,' said one senior climate expert.

Although the final wording of the report is still being worked on, the draft indicates that scientists now have a clearest idea so far about future climate changes, as well as about recent events. It points out that 12 of the past 13 years were the warmest since records began; ocean temperatures have risen at least three kilometres beneath the surface; glaciers, snow cover and permafrost have decreased in both hemispheres; sea levels are rising at the rate of almost 2mm a year; and cold days, nights and frost have become rarer while hot days, hot nights and heat waves have become more frequent.

And the cause is clear, say the authors: 'It is very likely that man-made greenhouse gas increases caused most of the average temperature increases since the mid-20th century,' says the report. **To date** these changes have caused global temperatures to rise by 0.6C. The most likely **outcome** of continuing rises in greenhouse gases will be to make the planet a further 3C hotter within 10 years' time, although the report acknowledges that rises of 4.5C to 5C could be experienced. Ice-cap melting, rises in sea levels, flooding, cyclones and storms will be an inevitable consequence.

Past assessments by the IPCC have suggested such scenarios are 'likely' to occur this century. _Its_ latest report, based on sophisticated computer models and more detailed observations of snow cover loss, sea level rises and the spread of deserts, is far more robust and confident. Now the panel writes of changes as 'extremely likely' and 'almost certain'. And in a specific rebuff to sceptics who still argue natural variation in the Sun's output is the real cause of climate change, the panel says mankind's industrial emissions have had five times more effect on the climate than any **fluctuations** in solar radiation. _We_ are the masters of our own destruction, **in short**.

There is some comfort, however, if you live in the British Isles. The panel believes that the Gulf Stream will continue to have a warming effect on the islands for at least another 100 years, keeping the climate temperate and mild all year-round. It was thought that melting ice pouring off Greenland's glaciers could have weakened the warm current and potentially plunged much of Western Europe into a mini Ice Age, just as depicted in the disaster film _The Day After Tomorrow_ – a scenario perhaps even more devastating than global warming itself. But, thankfully, it looks like that will not be the case.

The report reflects climate scientists' growing fears that the Earth is nearing the stage when atmospheric carbon dioxide level rises will bring **irreversible** change to the planet. 'We are seeing **vast** sections of Antarctic ice disappearing at an **alarming** rate,' said one climate expert. 'That means we can expect to see sea levels rise by about a metre a century from now on - and that will have devastating consequences.' However there is still hope, said Peter Cox, a college lecturer. 'We are like alcoholics who have got as far as admitting there is a problem. _It_ is a start. Now we have got to start drying out - which means reducing our carbon output.'

Second Reading

C. Using your own words as far as possible, answer the questions by reading and interpreting the meaning of the text.

. Do you think marine life will be killed off? If yes, why?

_____

. Why is the document described as 'very conservative'? (para 2)

_____

. Why is the IPCC's latest report its most accurate?

_____

. What do some sceptics believe?

_____

. What will happen when carbon dioxide reaches a certain level?

_____

D. Say what the underlined words in italics refer to in the text.

   1. 'others' (para 2)   _____

   2. 'Its' (para 5)   _____

   3. 'We' (para 5)   _____

   4. 'It' (para 7)   _____

Vocabulary in context

E. Find a word or expression in bold in the text that has the same meaning as (or a similar meaning to) each of the following:

1. look at something very carefully _____

2. up till now _____

3. worrying _____

4. constant small changes in something _____

5. briefly _____

6. escape from a place _____

7. wealthy _____

8. result _____

9. large _____

10. unable to be changed back _____

F. Use the correct form of the words below to complete the sentences. All the words have been taken from the text.

| spread | strain | reflect | depict | disrupt |
| plunge | chill | robust | devastate | prevalent |

1. The tsunami had a .... effect on the villages along the coast.

2. The fact that he can't find a job is .... their relationship.

3. The country was .... into war after the island was invaded.

4. Train services have been badly .... by the cow on the tracks.

5. He told us the .... story of how he was nearly killed in a car crash.

6. The story of his life was .... in the film.

7. The disease has .... all over the country.

8. Shark attacks are .... in these waters so be very careful.

9. His .... business plan impressed the bank manager.

10. His speech .... his interest in music.

Class discussion

It is the responsibility of schools to educate children so that they learn how to protect the environment.
What are your thoughts on this statement'?

Refer back to Unit 3 for tips on answering Short Answer questions. As always, read the passage first for gist, then can to locate the relevant sections and read those sections carefully to ensure you answer correctly.

uestions 1 – 6

nswer the questions below.

oose **NO MORE THAN THREE WORDS** from the passage for each answer.

1: A draft copy of the Fourth Assessment Report shows that the frequency of devastating storms will do what?

_____

2: What will global warming create as hundreds of millions of people flee their homes?

_____

3: The draft IPCC report indicates that scientists have their clearest idea yet about recent events and what else?

_____

4: At what rate are sea levels now rising each year?

_____

5: What man-made phenomenon probably caused most of the average temperature increases since the mid-20th century?

_____

6: For how much longer is the Gulf Stream expected to follow its present path?

_____

Refer to Unit 3 for tips on doing *Identification of writer's views/claims or information in the text* task types. Scanning will help you locate the relevant section of the passage. Careful reading will be required to help you decide whether or not the statements are valid.

Questions 7 – 10

Do the following statements agree with the information given in the reading passage?

> **TRUE** if the statement agrees with the information
>
> **FALSE** if the statement contradicts the information
>
> **NOT GIVEN** if there is no information on this

ANSWER

7: The latest IPCC report is based on computer models that have accounted for all variables. _____

8: Writers of the report believe natural variation in the Sun's output is the real cause of climate change. _____

9: *The Day After Tomorrow* was a disastrously bad film and a box office flop. _____

10: Scientists are worried by the rate at which huge sections of polar ice are melting. _____

> Notes/Table/Summary/Flow-chart Completion task tips were provided in Unit 5. Questions 11-14 below will require careful reading.

Questions 11 – 14

Complete the following summary of the final paragraph using the words A-H from the box below.

> **A: doubtful**   **B: high**   **C: expected**   **D: rising**
>
> **E: going**   **F: disastrous**   **G: positive**   **H: hopeful**

Scientists are increasingly fearful that 11_____ levels of atmospheric carbon dioxide will bring irreversible change to the planet. Sea levels are 12 _____ to rise by about a meter a century from now on. This could have 13_____ consequences. However, scientists are 14_____ as the willingness to reduce our carbon footprint now exists.

Vocabulary

Vocabulary

A. Study the text to try to understand the meaning of the words in bold.

Ecosystems fight back

Goat Island, off the northeastern coast of New Zealand's North Island, is one of the country's most popular marine-based tourist attractions. One of the few areas of the country's waters where it's easy to see wildlife in **abundance**, this marine reserve **draws** thousands of visitors every year. It also stands as a **prime** example of how the collapse of an ecosystem can be reversed by protecting biodiversity.

Overfishing during the mid-20th century caused a significant loss of biodiversity in many of New Zealand's coastal ecosystems. This, in turn, eroded the **resilience** of the marine ecosystem. In many cases, including the area around Goat Island, a decline in populations of **predators** caused a huge increase in sea urchins, which in turn reduced the kelp forests that provide an important habitat for many other species.

The turning point for Goat Island came in 1975, when it became New Zealand's first marine reserve. Gazetted for scientific study, it was **designated** a no-take zone, and its wildlife received full protection. Once the new regulations were **imposed**, the situation changed dramatically. The ecosystem gradually began to recover, thanks to the **resurgence** of predators such as snapper and spiny lobster. Urchin densities **declined** by up to 70 per cent, which **enabled** the kelp to re-establish itself and this, in turn, enabled the return of its associated range of species.

The successful conservation of Goat Island has benefited more than just its wildlife. It **galvanised** support for a network of marine reserves around the country and it has given people an idea of the value of ecosystems in general, because thousands of people every year **flock** to these reserves to view the wildlife. There is a lot at stake here and the local community appreciates that.

B. Complete the sentences with the correct form of one of the words in bold from the text.

1. The company was .... into taking the necessary action when its profits fell drastically.

2. This is a(n) .... example of how a little help can go a long way.

3. The funding will .... them to buy the new equipment that they need for the juvenile centre.

4. There has been a(n) .... of violence in the city centre after the police beat a group of rioters.

5. Thousands of people .... to see the movie star when she went to the premiere.

6. The lion is the main .... of animals such as antelope and elephants.

7. His body's .... to infection has been weakened by the illness.

8. There is a(n) .... of good restaurants in this neighbourhood so we are spoiled for choice.

9. The .... in industry has led to mass unemployment in this area.

10. This part of the restaurant has been .... a no-smoking area.

11. The workers aren't happy about the new rules that are being .... on them.

12. The national park .... thousands of visitors every year.

C. Complete each sentence with a suitable form of one of the words in the box below to make an idiom. Some of the words may be used more than once.

world	earth	rain	spring	air	moon	grass	cloud

1. He was full of the joys of .... when Jenny agreed to go on a date with him.

2. People are never satisfied with what they've got as the .... is always greener on the other side.

3. She was on .... nine after passing the exam.

4. I don't know what we are going to do as everything is still up in the .... at the moment.

5. What on .... do you think you are doing?

6. I know you are disappointed, but it's not the end of the ....

7. It's one problem after another. It never .... but it pours.

8. The team was over the .... to win the competition.

9. The new person at work knows my brother. It's a small ....

10. I'm not surprised he didn't do well as he seems to have his head in the .... most of the time.

Nouns from phrasal verbs

D. Phrasal verbs can be made into nouns such as 'breakdown' or 'drawback'. Look at the nouns below and choose the correct definition.

1. The **outcome** of something is
   a. an attitude
   b. a start or beginning
   c. an exit
   d. the result

2. An **overseer** is
   a. a tall building
   b. a careless mistake
   c. a manager or supervisor
   d. a sudden flood

3. A **drawback** is
   a. a bridge over a river or moat
   b. a disadvantage
   c. a defeat
   d. a financial refund

4. A **tip-off** is
   a. money given to a waiter/waitress
   b. an open truck for carrying things
   c. a place where garbage is left
   d. information (given to the police)

5. An **outburst** is
   a. a sudden expression of emotion
   b. matching clothes
   c. a store
   d. a large amount of money spent on something

6. **Turnover** is
   a. the number of people who attend an event
   b. a change of direction
   c. a place where one road leads off from another
   d. sales over a certain period of time

7. A **breakthrough** is
   a. depression
   b. when someone goes into a property illegally or by force
   c. a discovery or success (after a lot of effort)
   d. a serious accident

8. An **outlet** is
   a. a place where things can be bought
   b. a criminal
   c. your attitude towards something
   d. the edge of something

E. Use the correct form of the words above to complete the sentences below.

1. There has been a major .... in the treatment of cancer over the last few years.

2. There are several .... in town where you can buy jeans cheaply.

3. One of the .... of this job is that I have to work every weekend.

4. The robbers were caught after a secret ....

5. Our store's .... has increased since we spent more money on advertising.

6. In a sudden .... of anger, she told him that she hated him.

7. It's the job of the .... to ensure that everyone is working properly.

8. No matter what the .... of the test is, I will support you.

Reading - 2

The purpose of this next section is to give students further practice in Diagram Labelling.
Read the text once first to get a general understanding. When doing the labelling tasks, you will
first have to scan the text to find the relevant sections and then read these sections carefully to
get the right answers.

The Perfect Storm

It all begins deep beneath the earth's surface in the mantle where powerful
forces are at work. The extreme temperatures in the earth's interior create
magma – melted or liquid rock. The magma rises towards the surface and
forces its way inside the earth's crust – the solid rock nearest the surface.
Here it builds up in a magma chamber. Enormous pressure is exerted on
the surrounding rock and eventually the magma blasts or melts a conduit (channel) in a fractured or weakened
part of the rock. As the magma nears the surface, the gas in the magma is released. The gas and magma blast
out an opening called the central vent. Some magma and gas may also escape through smaller side vents in the
mountain. The magma erupts as gas, lava, dust and other fragments. Lava flows may roll down the mountain,
but the most dangerous eruptive material is a combination of gas and dust, avalanches of which can sweep
down the mountainside at incredible speeds, engulfing everything in their path.

But as if the initial impact of a volcanic eruption wasn't bad enough, large-scale eruptions actually have consequences which reach far beyond the immediate vicinity of the eruption site itself and the fallout zone which is
affected by ash clouds and volcanic material. And with the recent surge in volcanic activity in Iceland, which
has seen two major eruptions in just over a year, and signs that more eruptions could be on the way, it is
exactly these more widespread consequences that scientists are becoming concerned about - and the fear that
we could be in for the perfect storm.

Already, some climatologists are concerned about the effect global warming is having on the northern
European climate, and, paradoxically, the way in which it may, in the long run, actually make parts of Europe
extremely cold. The fear is that melting Arctic ice could interfere with the North Atlantic Drift, a precious
warm current, and an offshoot of the Gulf Stream (which carries warm water in a circular flow from the Gulf
of Mexico to Europe and back again). At present, the North Atlantic drift effectively insulates parts of
Northern Europe, keeping winter temperatures, in the British Isles for example, several degrees above other
land masses at similar latitudes in other parts of the world. The problem is that cold water entering the sea as
the ice melts may strengthen the Labrador Current (a cold-water current which flows around Greenland and
down the coast of eastern Canada), which, in turn, may cause the path of the North Atlantic Drift to shift, or,
worse still, cause the flow of warm water to disappear completely, possibly plunging parts of Europe into a
mini ice-age.

Now, the perfect storm scenario arises if, at the same time as the North Atlantic Drift weakens, there is an
upsurge in volcanic activity - which brings us back to Iceland. There is, you see, a direct link between temperature and the amount of volcanic activity that has occurred; the more volcanically active a year it has been, the
more likely the following winter is to be a severe one, as volcanic activity creates cloud and ash cover, which is
one of the most potent ways of cooling the Earth. Few scientists are predicting this doomsday scenario with
any confidence yet, and the climate is exhibiting such volatility at the moment that any kind of prediction is
proving challenging. However, there is, nonetheless, a noticeable angst among scientists over what could happen next.

A. Look at the diagram of an erupting volcano below. Refer back to the text to find the information you need, then fill in labels 1-6. Use **NO MORE THAN TWO THREE WORDS** for each answer.

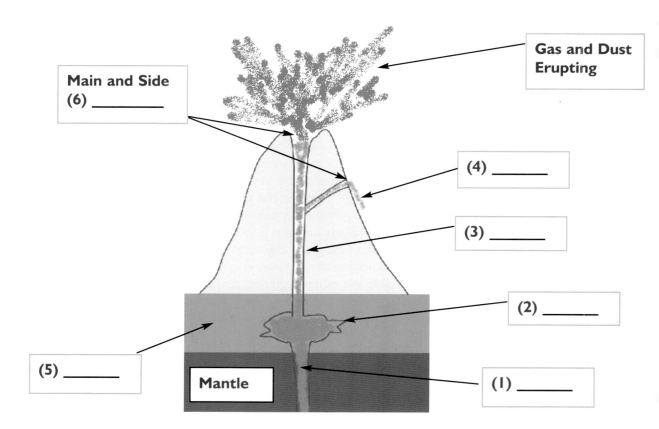

Gas and Dust Erupting

Main and Side (6) _____

(4) _____

(3) _____

(2) _____

(5) _____

Mantle

(1) _____

B. The diagram below shows the three main currents discussed in the text. Label the currents correctly. Use **NO MORE THAN THREE WORDS** for each answer.

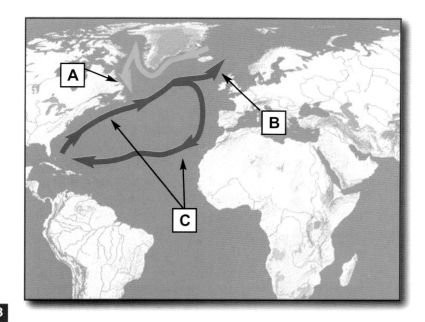

(1)   **A:** _____

(2)   **B:** _____

(3)   **C:** _____

UNIT 8 — Technological Advances

Lead In

A.

- What do you consider to be the most useful piece of technology in your house and why?
- How much do computers affect your life?
- Which historical invention would you most like to have invented and why?

B. Use the correct form of the words in the box below to complete the sentences. All the words are connected in some way with technology and inventions.

signal	surf	patent	gadget	interfere
install	transmit	wireless	spam	circuit

1. The thief was caught on film by the closed .... TV cameras.

2. I enjoy .... the web and looking for interesting wildlife sites on the internet.

3. Whenever I go to send an email, I have a load of .... to delete first.

4. It's great having .... internet as I can use my laptop in any room in the house.

5. I can't get a good enough .... here to use my mobile phone.

6. Use of electronic devices is forbidden because of possible .... with the plane's computer systems.

7. You should take out a(n) .... on your invention so that no one can copy it.

8. We have just had a new security system .... in our workplace.

9. This is a very useful .... for opening cans and bottles.

10. The Olympic Games are .... by satellite to countries all over the world.

Reading -1

Pre-reading

A. Can you think of situations where robotics are used?

_____

Do you believe that robots will be used more or less in the future?

_____

Do you think it will ever be possible for robots to think for themselves and make decisions?

_____

B. Group Work

Now, look at the images below. Do you think it is likely that robots will be able to perform these roles in the future? What other things might robots be able to do many years from now? Are there some things robots will never be able to do?

Child-minding

Robot Pets

Having Relationships

Cleaning

Robot Police

Going to war

First Reading

C. Scan the text to find the information.

1. Where does Ronald Fearing work? _____
2. How wide will the 'robobugs' be? _____
3. Where were the latest flying robots recently on display? _____
4. Why is the device developed by Conn too heavy to take off? _____

The Mechanical Insect

A In 1804 George Cayley installed a **bizarre** machine at the top of his staircase. He attached wings of various shapes to a whirling arm atop the device, and as it spun the wings would either climb or descend depending on their ability to generate lift. This helped Cayley to develop the aerodynamic theories that led to his highly successful manned glider flights, and **ultimately** to the Wright brothers' powered aircraft.

B More than two centuries later, a whirling arm is once again being used to prepare the next revolution in flight technology: micro-aircraft that harness the complex aerodynamics and **navigation** techniques of insects. In his lab at the University of California, Berkeley, micro-systems engineer Ronald Fearing fixes each new version of the mechanical insect he is developing to the tip of a 30cm free-spinning arm he calls a "flight mill". Like Cayley's machine, this allows him to measure how much lift his creation can generate, and to test different ways of controlling it.

C Mechanical insects could prove far more manoeuvrable than micro-sized versions of **conventional** aircraft or helicopters. The insect-like craft could fly **unobtrusively** around buildings, zipping into open windows, for example. When equipped with different kinds of sensors, they could be used as miniature spy drones, security guards and pollution monitors.

D The military in particular is interested. The Pentagon's Defense Advanced Research Projects Agency (DARPA) is developing four flying "robobugs", weighing up to 10 grams each and with wingspans of up to 7.5cm. One of the two companies developing the craft for DARPA - Aerovironment, based in Monrovia, California, aims to have a "rough demonstrator" flying by the middle of next year.

E It is challenging work. If micro-aircraft like Fearing's are ever to fly, they will not only need to generate lift in a similar way to bugs but also sense their environment to allow them to maintain stability and land safely. Recent developments in wing mechanics and control systems mean that researchers are now getting close. The first **hurdle** for engineers like Fearing is to develop mechanisms that will generate enough lift. Insects do this by **rapidly** beating their wings down and forward, and then rotating them back and upward. At last week's Society for Experimental Biology meeting in Glasgow, UK, a **host** of new robotic insect-wing designs and flapping mechanisms were on display. Andrew Conn at the University of Bristol in the UK unveiled a hummingbird-sized wing mechanism driven by a pair of motorised aluminium cranks that reproduce a typical insect wing beat: one crank beats the 7.5cm wing up and down, while the other rotates it. Unlike previous mechanisms, says Conn, the current design's wing **motion** is adjustable and should allow more manoeuvrability in the air.

F However, the team, which is being funded by the UK government's Defence Science and Technology Laboratory, has found that friction in the mechanism is slowing the wing's beating. The device is also currently too heavy to take off, so the researchers plan to replace as much metal as possible with carbon fibre. "We'll probably need to halve our weight and at least triple our lift," says Conn.

G At the Swiss Federal Institute of Technology in Lausanne, flight researcher Dario Floreano is already testing optical-flow sensing software on a miniature propeller-driven aircraft. Dubbed Microflyer tracks the position of features on the ground and walls using two cameras scanning below and ahead. The aircraft may not look much like a bug but it certainly flies like one, he says. "The way that it behaves, changes direction, avoids walls and moves indoors is just like the way a housefly moves," says Floreano. If robotic insects do fly, Fearing believes they will quickly become cheap and **commonplace**. "Something that weighs less than a tenth of a gram will sell for less than a buck," he says.

Second Reading

D. Choose the correct answer A, B, C or D to answer the questions.

1. **George Cayley**
   A. was the first international pilot.
   B. tried to fly with wings attached to his arms.
   C. was a pioneer in aviation technology.
   D. was inspired by the Wright brothers.

2. **Which of the following is not mentioned as a potential use for mechanical insects?**
   A. discreet surveillance
   B. transportation
   C. environmental issues
   D. spotting a security breech

3. **According to Conn, his new design**
   A. will be very effective after some modifications.
   B. has different parts that can be attached to it.
   C. needs to have bigger wings attached to it.
   D. has the appearance of an insect.

4. **The microflyer**
   A. can see all around itself at any one time.
   B. is sensitive to solid objects around it.
   C. is very easy and cheap to produce.
   D. has two cameras that look like the eyes of a housefly.

5. **From the text, one can conclude that robotics**
   A. is a scientific field with a limited lifespan.
   B. technology is too expensive to be used widely.
   C. technology has very little relevance in the modern world.
   D. is developing successfully as a scientific field.

Vocabulary in context

E. Find a word or expression in bold in the text that has the same meaning as (or a similar meaning to) each of the following:

1. obstacle; problem   _____
2. movement   _____
3. strange; unusual   _____
4. the act of directing the course of a journey   _____
5. found everywhere   _____
6. in the end; finally   _____
7. a product or method that is usually used or has been used for a long time   _____
8. quickly   _____
9. discreetly, without drawing attention   _____
10. a large group or number of something   _____

F. Use the correct form of the words below to complete the sentences. All the words have been taken from the text.

| generate | man | harness | zip |
| rotate | unveil | track | scan |

1. George quickly .... through the traffic on his motorcycle.

2. Helicopter propellers .... quickly to lift the helicopter into the air.

3. The police .... the robbers' movements as they tried to escape down the highway.

4. The secret plan will be .... at the meeting on Friday.

5. I pulled over when I saw the .... car rolling down the hill towards me on the wrong side of the road.

6. The politician proposed to .... the power of the river to make electricity.

7. I .... the faces in the crowd but I couldn't see her.

8. We need to .... more interest in the project so that more people can support it.

Class discussion

As a class, discuss situations where robots can be particularly useful. Think particularly about industry, security and the emergency services.

Locating information – refer back to Unit 4 for tips. Remember, you should skim for gist to have a general understanding of the subject of each paragraph. You may then have to scan for specific information and read carefully for detail.

Questions 1 – 10

This reading passage has seven paragraphs, A-G. Read the passage and decide which paragraph contains the following information. Write the correct letter A-G in the answer section.
NB You may use any letter more than once.

		ANSWER
1:	how friction can affect wing beating	_____
2:	how robotic insects will quickly become inexpensive and common	_____
3:	that the first difficulty for engineers working on micro-aircraft is to generate enough lift.	_____
4:	how flying robobugs are being developed for defence purposes	_____
5:	that micro-aircraft may weigh less than a tenth of a gram	_____
6:	that a man installed a strange machine on top of a staircase	_____
7:	how small aircraft can fly unnoticed around buildings	_____
8:	the advantage of miniature flying machines over normal aircraft and helicopters	_____
9:	how, after 200 years, the next revolution in flight technology is being prepared	_____
10:	how theories were developed that led to successful glider flights and powered aircraft	_____

Multiple choice – refer to Unit 1 for tips on doing multiple choice questions. The question below will test your overall understanding of what this passage is about – the gist of the passage.

Question 11
Choose the correct answer A,B, C, or D. There is one correct answer.

11:     What would be a suitable title for this passage?

A: Scientists learn from insects

B: The defence department's deadliest weapon

C: The future of passenger aircraft

D: Spying on ordinary people

Refer back to Unit 3 for tips on answering Short Answer questions. Scan to locate the relevant sections and read carefully to ensure you answer the questions below correctly.

Questions 12-14
Answer the questions below.
Choose NO MORE THAN THREE WORDS from the passage for each answer.

12:   What did George Cayley install at the top of his staircase?

_____

13:   What is the Pentagon's Defense Advanced Research Projects Agency developing?

_____

14:   What is Andrew Conn's hummingbird-sized wing mechanism driven by?

_____

Vocabulary

A. Study the text to try to understand the meaning of the words in bold.

Einstein - a man of strong principles

In February 1950, a few months after the Soviet Union exploded its first atomic bomb and just after President Truman announced that the US would **accelerate** the production of a "super" (hydrogen) bomb, Albert Einstein went on nationwide US television to drop his own bombshell. "If these efforts should prove successful," he told his fellow Americans, "radioactive poisoning of the atmosphere and, **hence**, **annihilation** of all life on Earth will have been brought within the range of what is technically possible." He also warned of a malaise in the country: "**Tremendous** financial power is being concentrated in the hands of the military; youth is being militarised; and the loyalty of citizens, particularly civil servants, is carefully supervised by a police growing more powerful every day."

The very next day, J. Edgar Hoover, director of the FBI, sent a top-secret memo to every FBI office in the country requesting any and all "**derogatory** information" they had on Einstein. Hoover's efforts to prove that the world's most famous scientist was a Communist sympathiser - perhaps an "atom spy" and to have him **deported** from his adopted country would continue for the rest of Einstein's life. When the FBI's file was closed after his death in 1955, it contained more than 1800 pages of public statements by him and **unsubstantiated** allegations against him. The investigation remained secret until the 1990s. Even now, this aspect of Einstein's extraordinary life often **provokes** surprise and discomfort.

Einstein scholars and biographers have tended to **downplay** their subject's political activism in favour of his awe-inspiring scientific achievements and **tumultuous** personal life. The only substantial books on his politics published in English have been collections of his own writings which are **shorn** of their historical context. The main reason for this gap in the literature seems to be that Einstein's interventions in politics were not decisive - with the single, **crucial** exception of the letter he wrote in August 1939 to President Roosevelt **urging** him to set up a government inquiry into the possibility of building an atomic bomb. What's more, Einstein's politics have widely been **regarded** as naive. He **fervently** campaigned for a world government - or a reformed United Nations - with the military power to enforce the settlement of **disputes** between nations and thereby to abolish war. These positions earned him a reputation for being a wide-eyed and largely irrelevant **idealist**.

To complicate matters, Einstein never joined a political party or movement, making it difficult for any group to claim him as its own. His closest links were with the Zionists in the 1920s and the Pacifists in the 1930s; yet in both cases there was a public falling-out, most **notably** with the Pacifists in 1933, after Hitler's rise to power when Einstein **abruptly** changed his mind about compulsory military service and supported it as a necessary **bulwark** against German rearmament.

B. Complete these sentences with the correct form of one of the words in bold in the text.

1. She .... her son to reconsider when he told her that he didn't want to stay at college.

2. He .... denied that he'd been involved in the robbery.

3. She is .... as one of the leading poets of her time.

4. The trouble with being a(n) .... is that you are bound to be disappointed in the end.

5. Isn't there some way that we can .... the process as I need an answer quickly.

6. We need an unbiased mediating service to settle the .... between the workers and the management.

7. It's .... that you hand in the work before the deadline.

8. He tends to .... the seriousness of the problem because he is in denial.

9. The newspaper was sued for printing .... stories about his corrupt activities.

10. The men were .... because they did not have the necessary papers to work or live in this country.

11. They .... withdrew their offer when they found out that he was a criminal.

12. The critic's .... remarks about the new play have affected its popularity.

C. Number idioms
Complete each of the idiomatic expressions with a suitable word from the box below. Some words may be used more than once.

eleventh	two	second	sixth	one	first	twice	halved	nine

a. It is .... to none.

b. Well, back to square ....

c. He is on cloud ....

d. .... wrongs don't make a right.

e. It is .... nature.

f. I have a .... sense about it.

g. It was at the .... hour.

h. On .... thoughts . . .

i. I don't know the .... thing about it.

j. After all, a trouble shared is a trouble ....

k. .... can play at that game.

l. That would kill .... birds with one stone.

D. Using the proverbs and expressions above. Think of suitable responses to the statements below.

1. I'm so worried. I need someone to talk to.

2. So you think this is the best restaurant in town, do you?

3. You don't know how to fix a jammed printer, do you?

4. Now we've got to think up a new plan as that was a complete failure.

5. We were lucky that John arrived with the money just in time.

6. George must be thrilled to have passed all his exams.

7. How did you know that it was going to be Ben on the phone?

8. Greg learned to play the piano quickly, didn't he?

9. Why are you so obsessed with getting your revenge for what he did?

10. Did you see that? He just threw his garden rubbish into our garden.

11. I've got a nice evening planned for us. We are going to clean the house when you come round.

12. We could go to the library on the way to the store.

E. The words in the box labelled 'Antonym' are opposite in meaning to the words marked in bold in the original text. Find the words of opposite meaning in the original text and write them in the 'Word from Text' column next to their antonym. (Not all the words in bold in the original text will be needed.)

Antonym	Word from Text
Peaceful	Tumultuous
Talk up	_____
Agreements	_____
Dissuading	_____
Complimentary	_____
Welcomed	_____
Preservation	_____

Antonym	Word from Text
Confirmed	_____
Gradually	_____
Trivial	_____
Indifferently	_____
Realist	_____
Delay	_____
Inconsiderable	_____

F. Now, using suitable words from the 'Antonym' column above, fill in the gaps in sentences 1 - 10. (You will not need all the words.)

1. Apple yesterday .... newspaper reports that a new version of the iphone 5 will be released nex March.

2. The South Korean government has invested a not .... amount of money in the project, so it is hoped that the placing of robot-guards in prisons will prove a successful experiment.

3. We must not allow the progress of technology to continue apace if this progress is to the detriment of the natural world, the .... of which should be our number one priority.

4. A .... protest was held by students unhappy with the government's announcement of cuts in the research and technology budget being afforded to top universities.

5. The government continues to .... its year-old scheme to encourage students to study the sciences, despite the fact that all evidence suggests it is not working.

6. The U.N. is drafting a treaty on the ethical use of technology; the problem is such .... rarely receive unilateral support.

7. .... people from buying petrol-guzzling cars is the difficult task facing the new Minister for Transport, though the challenge has just been made somewhat easier with the announcement of a new hybrid vehicle capable of matching the performance of petrol-fuelled models.

8. There is too much hype surrounding the potential of this new technology; the voice of a .... is needed to keep everyone grounded.

9. Robotic technology is .... replacing manpower on production lines up and down the country.

10. The issue of whether it is okay to clone humans is far from .... ; it is one of the most fundamental questions mankind has ever faced.

Reading -2

Pre-Reading

A. Scan the text to find out what the following numbers represent.

1. 2000　　　2. 200 pounds　　　3. 705　　　4. 85 percent　　　5. 48 million

Advances in Lighting Technology

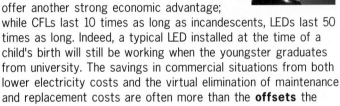

A The lighting **sector** is on the edge of a spectacular revolution, a shift from the century-old, inefficient incandescent light bulb to far more efficient technologies. Perhaps the quickest, most profitable way to reduce electricity use worldwide, thus cutting carbon emissions, is simply to change light bulbs.

B The first advance in this field came with compact fluorescent lamps, (called CFLs). Replacing the old-fashioned inefficient incandescent bulbs that are still widely used today with new CFLs can reduce the electricity used for lighting by three-quarters. And though a CFL may cost twice as much as an incandescent, it lasts 10 times as long. Each one reduces energy use compared with an incandescent by the **equivalent** of 200 pounds of coal over its lifetime. For perspective, the energy saved by replacing a 100-watt incandescent bulb with an equivalent CFL over its lifetime is **sufficient** to drive a Toyota Prius hybrid car from New York to San Francisco.

C It seems as if the world may be moving towards a political **tipping point** as the campaign to replace inefficient light bulbs **across the board** gathers pace. CFL production in China, which accounts for 85 percent of the world total, climbed from 750 million units in 2001 to 3 billion units in 2007. Of the estimated 4.7 billion light sockets in the United States, close to 1 billion now have CFLs. In February 2007, Australia announced it would **phase out** the sale of incandescents by 2010, replacing them with CFLs. Canada soon followed with a 2012 phaseout goal. In early 2009, the European Union (EU) also approved a phaseout of incandescent bulbs. Brazil, hit by a nationwide electricity shortage in 2000, responded with an **ambitious** programme to replace incandescents with CFLs. As a result, an estimated half of the light sockets there now contain these efficient bulbs. In 2007, China, working with the Global Environment Facility, announced a plan to replace all its incandescents with more-efficient lighting within a decade.

D CFLs contain a small amount of mercury (about one fifth the quantity in a watch battery), which has led to some environmental worries. Mercury is only released, however, if they are broken; if CFLs are handled carefully and safely recycled at the end of their useful lives, they are neither an environmental or health threat. Indeed, burning the coal needed to power one incandescent light bulb releases much more mercury into the atmosphere and eventually the water and food supply than the amount contained in a CFL.

E The second major advance in lighting technology is the light-emitting diode (LED), which has a number of advantages over CFL light bulbs. Most significantly, LEDs use up to 85 percent less electricity than an incandescent bulb - considerably less than a CFL even. LEDs offer another strong economic advantage; while CFLs last 10 times as long as incandescents, LEDs last 50 times as long. Indeed, a typical LED installed at the time of a child's birth will still be working when the youngster graduates from university. The savings in commercial situations from both lower electricity costs and the virtual elimination of maintenance and replacement costs are often more than the **offsets** the higher initial expense incurred.

F Although LEDs are the ultimate in lighting efficiency, they are still too costly for most uses. They are rapidly taking over several **niche** markets, however, such as traffic lights, where they now have 52 percent of the U.S. market, and exit signs in buildings, where they account for 88 percent of U.S. sales. New York City has replaced traditional bulbs with LEDs in many of its traffic lights, cutting its annual bill for maintenance and electricity by $6 million. In early 2009, Los Angeles Mayor Antonio Villaraigosa said the city would replace its 140,000 street lights with LEDs, saving taxpayers $48 million over the next seven years. The resulting reduction in carbon emissions would be like taking 7,000 cars off the road. Universities are also getting involved. In California, the University of California-Davis has a Smart Lighting Initiative. One of its first projects was to replace all the light bulbs in a campus parking garage with LEDs, dramatically reducing electricity use. This success has evolved into LED University, a project to **disseminate** LED technology. Early adopters include the University of California-Santa Barbara, Tianjin Polytechnic University in China, and the University of Arkansas.

G In summary, shifting to CFLs in homes, and to LEDs in traffic lights would cut the world share of electricity used for lighting from 19 percent to 7 percent. This would save enough electricity to close 705 of the world's 2,670 coal-fired plants. In a world facing almost daily new evidence of climate change and its consequences, a quick and **decisive** victory is needed in the battle to cut carbon emissions and stabilize the climate. A rapid shift to the most energy-efficient lighting technologies would provide just such a victory generating **momentum** for even greater advances in climate stabilization to come.

First Reading

B. Read the text again and then match up the paragraphs A-E with the most appropriate heading in the box below.

1. Paragraph **A**	
2. Paragraph **B**	
3. Paragraph **C**	
4. Paragraph **D**	
5. Paragraph **E**	
6. Paragraph **F**	
7. Paragraph **G**	

i.   How LED and CFL Technology Works
ii. LED Finding its Niche
iii. The Mercury Dilemma
iv. Drawbacks of the LED
v.   CFL Light Bulb Use Around the World
vi. A Light Revolution
vii. Shift to CFL and LED Today, for Tomorrow
viii. CFL Lighting Technology
ix. LED Lighting Technology

Second Reading

C. Read the text again and complete the chart and timeline below. Write no more than 2 words in each space.

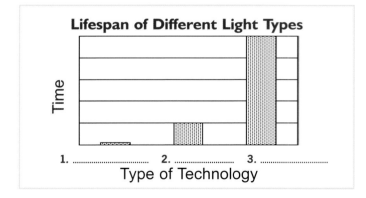

Lifespan of Different Light Types

Time / Type of Technology

1. .... 2. .... 3. ....

TIMELINE - Global Conversion to CFLs

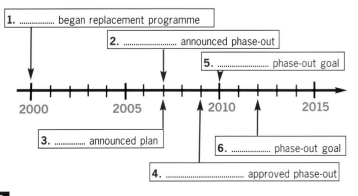

1. .... began replacement programme
2. .... announced phase-out
5. .... phase-out goal
3. .... announced plan
6. .... phase-out goal
4. .... approved phase-out

2000   2005   2010   2015

Vocabulary in context

D. Find a word or expression in bold in the text that has the same meaning as (or a similar meaning to) each of the following:

1. a specific area with particular characteristics _____
2. when a situation is true for everyone _____
3. significant or comprehensive _____
4. area of industry _____
5. to distribute something so that it reaches many people _____
6. something the same in size or function as something else _____
7. to gradually stop the use of something _____
8. speed of movement, becoming less likely to stop as speed increases _____
9. requiring great effort or representing a big challenge _____
10. the moment when things change direction _____
11. enough _____
12. counteracts the effect of another thing so that its advantage/disadvantage is lost _____

E. Use the correct form of the words from Exercise A above to complete the sentences.

1. Before becoming a teacher, he used to work in the financial ....
2. This recipe calls for a cup of milk. What is the .... in litres?
3. If your goal is too .... , you might not succee◖
4. The political system of this country has finally reached a .... ; everything has got to change.
5. The product was successful because it filled a vacant .... in the market.
6. The success of his first novel was a .... event i◖ John's life; he would never work as a salesman again.
7. If you want to learn, you must pay attention; simply turn up for class is not ....
8. Some businesses are now .... Windows, and◖ replacing it with open sourced, free software.
9. Jeans have revolutionised fashion .... ; they are worn on almost all occasions, all over the worl◖
10. News may now be .... instantly over the inter◖
11. He is critical but, in my opinion, his tendency to criticise .... by his immense knowledge.
12. The singer's career is picking up .... ; soon he'll be a superstar.

LEAD-IN

A.

• What kinds of crimes are committed in the area where you live?
• How safe do you feel where you live?
• Is there a high police presence where you live?
• How would you feel about a career in the police?

B. Pairwork

Look at the crimes in the box below. With your partner put the crimes in order of severity with the most serious first. Be prepared to justify your answers.

manslaughter	drink-driving	fraud	computer hacking
mugging	arson	speeding	shoplifting
identity theft	terrorism	hijacking	vandalism

Reading - 1

Pre-reading

A. Choose the correct word to complete each of the sentences below.

. The police have asked for any .... to the accident to come forward.
   A. viewers   B. spectators   C. witnesses   D. audiences

. The police car chased the criminals with its .... blaring.
   A. alarm   B. siren   C. horn   D. signal

. The jury took three hours to reach a ....
   A. conviction   B. sentence   C. punishment   D. verdict

. The building had to be .... because of the terrorist threat.
   A. discharged   B. unloaded   C. depleted   D. evacuated

. The .... denied stealing the man's money from his coat when he wasn't looking.
   A. pickpocket   B. blackmailer   C. shoplifter   D. burglar

. The youth was let out on .... until the court case in three weeks' time.
   A. custody   B. bail   C. internment   D. confinement

. The .... were held for several hours by the hijackers.
   A. hostages   B. prisoners   C. convicts   D. wardens

. The man was arrested for selling .... passports.
   A. artificial   B. double   C. forged   D. hoax

First Reading

B. Scan the text to find what the numbers below refer to.

1. 600   2. 18   3. 40   4. 38

A life of crime is bad for your health

A Antisocial behaviour doesn't just harm society - it may also harm the **perpetrator's** health. That's the message of a 30-year study examining the hidden costs of **petty** crime to society. The researchers, who monitored 600 children for 30 years, found that naughty boys who didn't reform in adulthood suffered worse health than their **peers**, many of whom were equally deprived in childhood. The researchers are now seeking a way of identifying those who are most likely to become **persistent** offenders, with a view to intervening before it is too late.

B "It's the first study to demonstrate the link between children who engage in antisocial behaviour and deficits in physical health when they grow up," says study leader Candice Odgers of the Institute of Psychiatry at King's College London. As well as accounting for more than their share of crime later in life, "they also incur **hitherto** unrecognised medical costs," she says.

C Odgers analysed data on more than 600 men in their early 30s, from a range of socio-economic backgrounds, in Dunedin, New Zealand. The results show that individuals whose bad behaviour began in childhood and persisted in adulthood were four times as likely to suffer from chronic bronchitis or gum disease as those who never engaged in bad behaviour. Although these individuals accounted for just 10 per cent of the sample, they were responsible for 18 per cent of traffic injuries, 29 per cent of the days spent in psychiatric hospitals, 72 per cent of the total months during which study members were homeless or taken in by others.

D Persistent offenders also had three times the healthy blood level of C-reactive protein, a marker that indicates a raised risk of heart attacks or stroke. "It is surprising to see this marked risk for heart disease in such young men", Odgers says. "As we follow them into their 50s and 60s, the health **burden** will likely get even worse." Her analysis so far provides strong data for determining who is most likely to offend, and their **subsequent** health. For example, 40 per cent of persistent offenders came from families of low economic status, and 23 per cent experienced maltreatment as a child - at least double that of any other group.

E Odgers' study reinforces previous research that early intervention could help. Around a quarter of the sample were badly behaved as children, but reformed in **adolescence**. Many of them had the same deprived backgrounds as the persistent offenders, yet by the age of 32 they were almost as healthy as the control group. The key question, says Odgers, is how to identify which boys are most likely to offend in later life. Possible markers include attention deficit hyperactivity disorder - which affected 38 per cent of persistent offenders - and a family history of alcohol addiction. Further analysis is under way to determine whether or not genes play a significant role in the propensity to become a repeat offender.

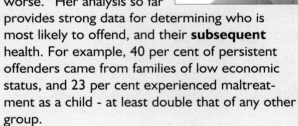

Second Reading

C. Say if the statements are True (T) or False (F) or Not Given (NG). Justify all your answers.

1. Being a naughty child usually leads to a life of crime.

2. Odgers is something of a pioneer in this particular area of research.

3. New Zealand has one of the highest juvenile crime rates in the world.

4. Financial difficulties can be a contributing factor in children turning to a life of crime.

5. There is evidence to show that juvenile delinquents can be helped to become well-behaved teenagers.

6. There is strong evidence to show that criminal tendencies are genetic.

Vocabulary in context

D. Find a word or expression in bold in the text that has the same meaning as (or a similar meaning to) each of the following:

1. happening again and again
2. teenage years
3. someone who commits a crime
4. people of the same group, age, class etc
5. not very serious or important
6. until now
7. following
8. something that causes difficulties or problems

E. Use the correct form of the words below to complete the sentences. All the words have been taken from the text.

> monitor   intervene   engage   incur   indicate
> determine   offend   reinforce   reform

1. If the boy .... again, he will probably be given a prison sentence.

2. We need to .... whether it is worth repairing the old car or if it would be better to buy a new one.

3. The police .... to stop the fight.

4. If you should .... any extra costs, we will refund you the money.

5. We can't prove that he has been .... in illegal activities.

6. The doctors are closely .... the woman's health.

7. If he doesn't .... his behaviour, he will end up leading a life of crime.

8. All the statistics .... that crime is decreasing in this area.

9. This spate of violent crimes .... the claim that more police are needed in the city.

Class discussion

Do you believe that parents should be punished if their child commits a crime? Discuss this issue as a class.

Choosing Headings for Paragraphs or Sections of a Text – refer to Unit 3 for detailed information on this type of task. Remember the questions below will test your general understanding – the gist – of each paragraph.

Questions 1 – 5

This reading passage has five sections, A-E.

Choose the correct heading for each section from the list of headings below.

List of Headings

i: Getting closer to the answer

ii: Comprehensive study reveals career criminals who start young suffer more health problems.

iii: Identifying and helping future offenders

iv: No clear link between childhood behaviour and later problems

v: Results of the study are mixed

vi: Persistent offenders prone to heart problems

vii: No hope for misbehaving children

viii: Childhood misbehaviour and adult health linked

ix: Government ignoring high crime rates

x: Antisocial behaviour – not good for anyone

1:	A :	_____
2:	B :	_____
3:	C :	_____
4:	D :	_____
5:	E :	_____

A life of Crime

Labelling a Diagram: The task below will require careful reading and is testing your ability to understand and visualise descriptions.

Questions 6-7

These questions are based on paragraph C. For the ten percent of the sample children whose bad behaviour persisted in adulthood, complete the labelling of the percentage bars in the graph below according to the details provided.

Bar C is labelled as an example. Label the other two bars correctly.
Example: *C: Total months spent homeless or taken in by others*

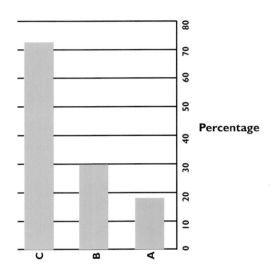

6:   A: _____

7:   B: days spent in _____

Notes/Tables/Summary/Flow-chart Completion – refer to Unit 5 for tips on how to complete this task type. Here you will be required to scan the passage to find the relevant section and then read carefully to get the correct answer.

Questions 8-14

Complete the notes below using NO MORE THAN TWO WORDS OR NUMBERS from the passage for each answer.

Notes on Institute of Psychiatry's research project:

Length of study: 8_____

Purpose for study: To examine the hidden costs of **9**_____ to society.

Number of subjects: 600

Findings:

- Clear link between children involved in antisocial behaviour and **10**_____ physical health when they grow up.

- Individuals whose bad behaviour began in childhood and persisted in adulthood were responsible for a disproportionately large number of minor offences and suffered more health problems.

- Repeat offenders more prone to **11**_____ or stroke.

- Many repeat offenders come from families of low **12**_____ or experienced maltreatment as a child.

- Possible early signs of potential persistent offenders include attention deficit **13**_____ and a family history of **14**_____ .

Vocabulary

A. Study the text to try to understand the meaning of the words in bold.

Is there a lawbreaker in us all?

Bad things are done by bad people. This, in a nutshell, is the philosophy behind just about all our social, political and religious institutions. The idea that, aside from mental illness and being too young to know better, people are free to choose how to behave and should be judged **accordingly,** is taken for granted pretty much all over the world.

Yet, things are not that simple, as evidence **amassed** by psychologists and social scientists shows. The message from this research is that sometimes badness comes from the situation, not the individual. People are far more strongly influenced by those around them than we like to think.

To take one extreme, most suicide bombers are ordinary, mentally fit and often educated people who are deliberately **manipulated** so that loyalty to a small group becomes **paramount** to them. Torturers too, are generally **indistinguishable** from the rest of the population. These people surrender responsibility to a higher authority and then follow orders.

"Situationist" mentality affects our everyday lives as well. You might think what you buy is your own decision, but in reality we are all influenced by the buying habits of others - a phenomenon responsible for the content of all those best-seller lists. And when people fear disrupting the **cohesion** of their group or committee, they may **withhold** important views that could lead to a better decision. This phenomenon, called groupthink, has been blamed for many **debacles**, including the loss of the space shuttle Columbia. No doubt it is responsible for countless poor decisions in business, political and social life; yet how many managers or committee chairs are aware of the dynamics involved?

The knowledge that we are not as free in our choices as we imagine raises a **host** of other questions. Just how do marketing companies, religious cults and political parties **wield** this influence? Does the fact that people are **swayed** by opinion polls mean that, in the interests of democracy, polls should be banned before elections? Among the most uncomfortable issues raised is the question of to what **extent** individuals are responsible for criminal acts they commit, and, for that matter, to what extent the courts should hold them culpable. Does the proper carriage of justice require that the influence, however direct or indirect, of groups over criminals should mitigate the criminals own culpability? To answer such questions and to **combat** suicide bombers and even genocide requires a better **grasp** of the influence of groups over individuals, and a determination to use that knowledge to positive **ends**.

B. **Complete the sentences with the correct form of the words in bold from the text.**

1. You must not .... information from the police if you believe it will help them with their investigation.

2. The strict teacher .... absolute power over the children in her classes.

3. It took me a long time to .... the Chinese language even though I lived there for a full nine years.

4. We need to .... as much information as we can when we start our new research project.

5. You should find out what the customs of the country are so that you can behave ....

6. I can think of a .... of reasons why you shouldn't date him.

7. Catching the violent criminal quickly is .... to the safety of the local community.

8. The engineers are assessing the .... of the damage to the building after the earthquake.

9. .... juvenile crime is a police policy.

10. Because teenagers tend to wear the same clothes, they are almost .... from each other.

11. If there is no .... within the team, we have no chance of winning the competition.

12. Don't let him .... you all the time. He is taking advantage of your good will.

13. We were .... by his intelligent argument because it made a lot of sense.

14. He has worked very hard, but to what ....? He still has nothing to show for it.

15. How will the politician escape being blamed for such a ....?

C. Same word - different meaning

Next to each of the following sets of sentences, you will find the meaning of the underlined words. Match the sentences (a, b, etc) with the correct meaning (1, 2, etc) in each set of sentences.

1. a) Why are you wearing <u>odd</u> socks?
   b) I've got a few <u>odd</u> jobs to do before I go out.
   c) It was rather <u>odd</u> that she phoned at three in the morning.
   d) Dave is the <u>odd one out</u> in our group.
   e) There were <u>forty-odd</u> people at the party.

   1. strange
   2. different from the rest
   3. one or two, not many, the number is not important
   4. approximately
   5. not matching

2. a) <u>Rich</u> food always gives me a stomach ache.
   b) A poet must have a <u>rich</u> vocabulary.
   c) "She said I'm fat!" "That's <u>rich</u> coming from her because she's enormous."

   1. high in fat or oily
   2. ironic
   3. large

3. a) You need to <u>face</u> the fact that she doesn't love you.
   b) The hotel <u>faces</u> the park.
   c) The politician had to <u>face</u> a lot of criticism from the media.

   1. is opposite/looks out on
   2. deal with
   3. accept

4. a) Can I <u>count on</u> you to be there if I need your help?
   b) <u>Don't count your chickens before they've hatched.</u>
   c) We hadn't <u>counted on</u> so many people coming to the wedding.

   1. expect/plan
   2. rely on
   3. don't expect sth good to happen until it is sure that it will

5. a) Don't forget to put a <u>pinch</u> of salt in the vegetables.
   b) I take everything that he says <u>with a pinch of salt</u>.
   c) He <u>pinched</u> his little sister and made her cry.

   1. not seriously
   2. small amount
   3. squash between two fingers

6. a) She phoned her friends in the <u>vain</u> hope that she may have left her keys at their house.
   b) He's so <u>vain</u> that he's always looking in the mirror.
   c) It was <u>in vain</u> that we tried to get her to change her mind.

   1. unsuccessfully
   2. unrealistic
   3. conceited

7. a) You need to clearly <u>state</u> what you really mean.
   b) Why is Bob in such a <u>state</u>?
   c) The President's body <u>lay in state</u> for two days before he was buried.
   d) In what kind of <u>state</u> are our finances this month?

   1. be in a public place for people to go and pay their last respects
   2. condition
   3. express/say
   4. negative mood/ be unstable, mentally upset

8. a) I'll <u>stick by</u> you no matter what happens.
   b. <u>Stick at it</u> and I'm sure it will get easier in time.
   c) <u>Stick</u> your bag on the floor for now.
   d) Do you think you can <u>stick</u> the two halves back together again?

   1. continue to do sth
   2. put
   3. fix/join
   4. support

D. Crime
Use the words in the box to complete the sentences.

1. The only reason he was charged with _____ and not murder is that the prosecution believe he acted in a fit of rage on learning of the affair the victim had with his wife – it was not premeditated.

2. He was convicted of first-degree _____ and the judge sentenced him to five life sentences – he will spend the rest of his days in jail.

3. Although the ordeal of the _____ left her in shock, at least she hadn't had any valuables on her person at the time – all he got from her was a five-pound note.

4. The man required forty stitches after the _____ , and was left with a black eye and two broken fingers.

5. The _____ scam was finally uncovered when bank notes were found hidden inside blocks of ice in the ship's hold.

6. The teenager was sentenced to community service for _____ ; the judge said he believed the accused person's hunger had driven him to take the sandwich.

7. _____ is rampant on the internet these days; more and more people are having their credit card details stolen and used by organised crime gangs that operate high-tech scams.

Manslaughter	**Money Laundering**
Assault	**Murder**
Mugging	**Shoplifting**
Fraud	

E. Punishment
Use the words in the box to complete the sentences.

1. The judge sentenced the man to a seven-year _____ in prison on account of the violent nature of the assault.

2. The _____ had not been handed down in this state for 22 years; however, given the terrible nature of the crime, the judge said he had no other option.

3. The notion of _____ is one which is always controversial; do we ever have the right to take someone's life no matter the seriousness of their crime?

4. The judge barred the man from applying for _____ for at least the first two years of his sentence.

5. The _____ in the case made the judge decide against sending the man to prison.

6. Although he was a repeat offender, the petty nature of the crime was the deciding factor in the defendant getting off with a _____.

term	**parole**
warning	**capital punishment**
mitigating circumstances	**death sentence**

F. Write 6 sentences using the words/phrases in the box above.

_____

_____

_____

_____

_____

_____

Reading - 2

Pre-Reading

A. Think about the questions below. Write short answers and then read the text.

1. What is free will?

2. Do you believe in fate?

3. How do you think the concept of free will might influence ideas about crime and law?

The Question of Free Will

I ought to tell you something concerning the question of free will. But you will understand that such a momentous question, which is worthy of a deep study of the many-sided physical, moral, intellectual life, cannot be summed up in a few short words. I can only say that the tendency of modern natural sciences, in physiology as well as psychology, has overruled the illusions of those who would persist in watching psychological **phenomena** merely within themselves and think that they can understand them without any other means.

On the contrary, positive science, backed by the testimony of anthropology and of the study of the environment, has arrived at the following conclusions: The **admission** of a free will is out of the question. For if the free will is but an illusion of our internal being, it is not a real **faculty** possessed by the human mind. Free will would imply that the human will, confronted by the choice of voluntarily making a certain decision, has the last decisive word under the pressure of circumstances **contending** for and against this decision; that it is free to decide for or against a certain course independently of internal and **external** circumstances, which play upon it, according to the laws of cause and effect.

If a man knows the principal causes which determine a certain phenomenon, he says that this phenomenon is **inevitable**. If he does not know them, he considers it as an accident, and this corresponds in the physical field to the **arbitrary** phenomenon of the human will which does not know whether it shall decide this way or that. For instance, some of us were of the opinion, and many still are, that the coming and going of meteorological phenomena was accidental and could not be foreseen. But in the meantime, science has demonstrated that they are likewise subject to the law of causality, because it discovered the causes which enable us to foresee their course. Thus weather prognosis has made wonderful progress with the help of a network of telegraphically connected meteorological stations, which succeeded in demonstrating the connection between cause and effect in the case of hurricanes, as well as of any other physical phenomenon. It is evident that the idea of accident, applied to physical nature, is unscientific. Every physical phenomenon is the necessary effect of the causes that determined it beforehand. If those causes are known to us, we have the **conviction** that that phenomenon is necessary - it is fate - and, if we do not know them, we think it is accidental.

The same is true of human phenomena. But since we do not know the internal and external causes in the majority of cases, we pretend that they are free phenomena, that is to say, that they are not **determined** necessarily by their causes. Hence the spiritualistic **conception** of the free will implies that every human being, in spite of the fact that their internal and external conditions are necessarily predetermined, should be able to come to a deliberate decision by the **mere** order of his or her free will, so that, even though the sum of all the causes demands a no, he or she can decide in favour of yes, and vice versa.

Now, who is there that thinks, when **deliberating** some action, what the causes are that determine his choice? We can justly say that the greater part of our actions are determined by habit, that we make up our minds almost from custom, without considering the reason for or against. When we get up in the morning we go about our customary business quite automatically, we perform it as a function in which we do not think of a free will. We think of that only in unusual and **grave** cases, when we are called upon to make some special choice, the so-called voluntary deliberation, and then we weigh the reasons for or against; we **ponder**, we hesitate about what to do.

Well, even in such cases, so little depends on our will in the deliberations which we are about to take that if anyone were to ask us one minute before we have decided what we are going to do, we should not know what we were going to decide. So long as we are undecided, we cannot foresee what we are going to decide; for under the conditions in which we live that part of the psychic process takes place outside of our consciousness. And since we do not know its causes, we cannot tell what its effects will be. Only after we have come to a certain decision can we imagine that it was due to our voluntary action. But shortly before we could not tell, and that proves that it did not depend on us alone.

Glossary: 1 free will: the belief that people have a choice in their actions, and that they are not determined in advance
2. fate: the belief that some power controls everything that happens in a way that cannot be prevented

First Reading

3. Do the following statements reflect the views of the writer in the reading passage? Write **YES** if the statement reflects the views of the writer, **NO** if the statement contradicts the views of the writer, and **NOT GIVEN** if it is impossible to say what the writer thinks about this.

1.	
2.	
3.	
4.	
5.	
6.	
7.	
8.	
9.	
10.	

. A complete account of the idea of free will will be put forward.

. Free will is a very important topic.

. A person's psychology comes completely from inside them.

. Science supports the idea of free will.

. It is impossible to predict the weather.

. Most people know the reasons for their decisions.

. Most people act out of habit.

. It is very important not to act out of habit.

. The fact that we cannot predict our decisions disproves free will.

0. Some people have more free will than others.

Second Reading

C. Choose the correct answer **A, B ,C or D** to answer the questions.

Free will is the ability to make a decision
A. without seeking the advice of others.
B. independent of one's circumstances.
C. with very little deliberation.
D. while accounting for the causes of that decision.

. To say something in nature is accidental
A. shows a deep understanding.
B. does not follow science.
C. means that it does not exist.
D. is proof of the existence of free will.

. If we understood the reasons for our decisions, we would
A. understand that there is no free will.
B. see the strength of free will.
C. no longer need to act on free will.
D. finally have the ability to use free will.

. People are most likely to think about a decision
A. that is customary.
B. that they don't understand.
C. that is unconscious.
D. that is serious.

Vocabulary in context

D. Find a word or expression in bold in the text that has the same (or a similar meaning) to each of the following definitions.

1. statement that something is true   _____

2. on or coming from the outside   _____

3. very serious and worrying   _____

4. certain to happen; cannot be avoided   _____

5. thinking about carefully before making a decision   _____

6. things that are observed to happen or exist   _____

7. used to emphasise how small or unimportant something is; simple   _____

8. to think about something carefully   _____

9. an idea of something formed in the mind   _____

10. competing for importance   _____

11. decided or settled   _____

12. a strong belief or opinion   _____

13. physical or mental ability   _____

14. not based on a plan or system   _____

E. Use the correct form of the words from Exercise **A** above to complete the sentences. You will not need to use every word.

1. After staying up all night, he did not have full use of his ....

2. Your .... of justice might not be the same as mine.

3. A tsunami is a frightening natural ....

4. Mark keeps his .... to himself because he dislikes arguments.

5. Although he was a .... child, he could sometimes say things that were remarkably wise.

6. His .... of love came too late; by that time she had already met someone else.

7. The .... financial forecasts are discouraging people from spending.

8. You should thoroughly .... over each of the various options.

9. Luck is .... ; you can't prepare yourself to be lucky.

10. Janice never finishes anything because she has so many projects .... for her time and attention.

11. If you park your car on that blind corner, it is .... that someone will hit it before long.

12. Neither doctor could .... the cause of his fatigue.

ead-In

Have you ever had to go to hospital? If so, how did you feel and how were you treated?
How would you feel about a career in the health professions?
What qualities do you think a person needs to have in order to be a nurse or doctor?

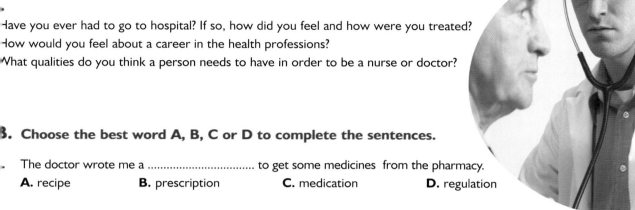

B. Choose the best word A, B, C or D to complete the sentences.

The doctor wrote me a .... to get some medicines from the pharmacy.
A. recipe   **B.** prescription   **C.** medication   **D.** regulation

You need a(n) .... diet in order to stay healthy.
A. stable   **B.** equal   **C.** balanced   **D.** steady

The doctors are very worried because the woman's health has .... overnight.
A. deteriorated   **B.** disintegrated   **C.** dissipated   **D.** dissolved

Are you ok? You look a bit off ....
A. colour   **B.** shade   **C.** tone   **D.** complexion

I must be allergic to the flowers because I have come out in a red .... all over my body.
A. freckle   **B.** rash   **C.** spot   **D.** bruise

You need to take a .... of this medicine four times a day with food.
A. portion   **B.** slice   **C.** sample   **D.** dose

The doctor couldn't feel a .... so she knew the man's heart had stopped beating.
A. flutter   **B.** throb   **C.** thump   **D.** pulse

I've got a .... headache. I think I'll take a painkiller.
A. crashing   **B.** splitting   **C.** drumming   **D.** ripping

Reading - 1

Pre-reading - Group Work

A. Talk together in small groups about which of the events in the box below are the most stressful and why. Come to an agreement about which are the three most stressful events. Be prepared to support and explain your views.

moving home	doing a job interview
getting married	taking an exam
going to the dentist	learning to drive
going to college	asking someone out on a date

First Reading

B. Scan the text and find the following information.

1. How many days sick leave can be blamed on stress annually?
2. What purpose does raised blood pressure have in an emergency?
3. If you are too stressed, what can happen if you injure yourself?
4. Why would working in a library be a stressful job?
5. What is 'commuter amnesia'?

Boiling point - the pressures of modern life

A Stress is the biggest occupational health problem in the developed world, say experts. A report by a mental health charity reveals that half of all workers now claim to suffer from stress and anxiety at work, resulting in the loss of nearly 13 million working days a year. The report says long hours, tough commutes and pressure to perform are frequently cited as leading causes of work stress. Away from the office it's not much better; many people working longer hours claim to do so to escape the pressures of family life. But are our modern-day lives really that much more **trying** than those of our **forebears**? And is stress necessarily bad for you?

B According to university professor Stafford Lightman, some **aggravation** - such as initial fear or panic - can be good news. If, say, you jump at the sudden appearance of a dog around a corner, you will experience a flood of stress hormones - first adrenalin and then cortisol - to prepare your body for fight, flight or fright. In such cases, becoming stressed is a basic survival instinct that triggers physiological responses needed for a quick getaway; blood pressure rises to allow blood to be pumped more quickly to your muscles, glucose is released for energy, and you become instantly more alert. And, even though we rarely need the fight or flight response to keep us alive in the modern world, it retains its usefulness. 'We still need it for survival in some respects,' says psychologist Dearbhla Mc Cullough. 'It's important to have our wits about us in this day and age - to avoid getting killed in traffic accidents, for instance.' Some people, such as athletes, thrive on a certain amount of stress in their lives. 'They need that release of hormones that comes from feeling **acutely** stressed in order to perform at their best,' McCullough says.

C This brief exposure to stress may actually help protect cells in the body against damage. Researchers have found that proteins triggered by **bouts** of stress in animals have a protective effect and help repair and eliminate cell damage caused by daily bodily processes. 'Sustained stress definitely is not good for you, but it appears that an occasional burst of stress or persistent low levels of stress can be very beneficial,' says Richard Morimoto, professor of biology at Northwestern University of Illinois.

D However, too much of a good thing spells trouble. It has long been proven by scientists that consistently high levels of cortisol generated by stress have numerous **adverse** effects on the body. Bodily repairs are overlooked, wounds take longer to heal and you become easily fatigued. People even become more **susceptible** to viruses as their immune response is impaired - studies have shown that the stressed are less likely to react positively to flu vaccines. Not to mention the fact that since more fatty acids and glucose are circulating in the bloodstream as stress continues to rise, the blood becomes viscous, which raises the risk of heart disease and diabetes.

E Lightman says that there are three reasons why some of us suffer more than others: our genes, our experiences in early life, and what's happened to us recently. Stressful events - getting married or divorced, changing jobs or moving house - are known to cause rising tension, but to what level is partly determined by our genetic stress thermostats. They have discovered that although our ability to deal with stress is determined at birth, it can change at various stages of life, including during early childhood.

F But it's not always the most obvious jobs that prove to be the most stressful. Presenting findings of a study at the annual conference of the British Psychological Society in Scotland earlier this year, Saqib Saddiq, a consultant with the recruitment company SHL, revealed that librarians experienced more stress than people working for the emergency services, driving a 125 mph express train, or teaching a class of challenging children. Saddiq interviewed 300 people in five occupations and found librarians to be most dissatisfied with their lot, and therefore more stressed. They complained that their jobs lacked variety and fulfilment, whereas, **remarkably**, members of the emergency services were happier and more relaxed at work. 'Although police officers and firefighters find themselves in stressful situations, there is much more variety in their work, both in terms of location and the type of work they do,' explains Saddiq.

G However, the study also confirmed that no occupation is immune to the effects of stress; one third of all respondents in Saddiq's trial suffered poor mental health because of work-related pressures, and anyone who commutes to work is likely to have those levels compounded. Dr David Lewis of the International Stress Management Association, believes commuting is a huge and significant cause of work-related stress. Two years ago he compared the blood pressure and heart rate of commuters with those of pilots and police officers taking part in **demanding** training exercises. Guess who felt more stressed? Whereas 'riot police or combat pilots have things they can do to combat stress that is being triggered by a particular event,' a commuter, particularly on a train, can do nothing at all,' he says. Indeed, stress is the reason that many people forget huge **chunks** of their journey to work, something Lewis has termed 'commuter amnesia'. There is this sense of helplessness combined with the stress that is perhaps the most worrying aspect of commuting.

Second Reading
C. Choose the correct answer A, B, C or D to answer the questions.

1. A recent report suggested that
A. most people have unhappy domestic lives.
B. people are working longer hours to avoid the rush hour commute.
C. people are too tired to perform well at work.
D. having to travel far to work can be unhealthy.

2. According to Dearbhla McCullough,
A. athletes suffer from extreme stress.
B. most people feel over-stressed when they are driving.
C. stress boosts our awareness of the situation we are in.
D. many road accidents are the result of extreme stress.

3. Which of the following is not mentioned as a negative result of stress?
A. general forgetfulness
B. vulnerability to viruses
C. suffering from exhaustion
D. possible cardiac disease

4. Lightman's research has shown that
A. there is nothing we can do if we are genetically vulnerable to stress.
B. early childhood is the time when we tend to be most stressed.
C. irrespective of our genetic inclination, we can alter the way that we deal with stress.
D. if we are to learn stress management, it must be in childhood.

5. According to Saddiq,
A. people who have stressful jobs, never get stressed.
B. being helpless in a situation is what causes most stress.
C. emergency services personnel use aggression to fight stress.
D. the terrible state of public transport is the main cause of stress.

Vocabulary in context

D. Find a word or expression in bold in the text that has the same meaning as (or a similar meaning to) each of the following:

1. difficult; causing a lot of worry or problems   _____
2. ancestors   _____
3. annoyance; irritation   _____
4. extremely   _____
5. a short period of time   _____
   (during which something unpleasant is experienced)
6. negative (in an extreme way)   _____
7. vulnerable to; easily affected by something   _____
8. surprisingly; unusually   _____
9. challenging; difficult   _____
10. piece or section of something   _____

E. Use the correct form of the words below to complete the sentences. All the words have been taken from the text.

cite	trigger	retain	thrive	eliminate
spell	impair	circulate	compound	term

1. If oxygen can't .... around the body, the brain will be damaged.
2. Do you know what .... his panic attack?
3. Your negative attitude will only .... the situation.
4. The presence of that rude boy always .... trouble.
5. We need to .... as many problems as we can from the system.
6. Children .... in a happy, safe family environment.
7. She managed to .... her sense of humour, even when the going got really tough.
8. His speech has been .... on account of damage he sustained to his mouth.
9. Doctors have .... this symptom, 'the nausea effect'.
10. He .... a few well-known examples of this phenomenon.

Class discussion

What do you do when you feel stressed?

Do you think it is better to be with lots of people or to take time out on your own when you feel anxious about something?

Exchange ideas on stress-busting activities.

In this final unit we will do a variety of different question types.

Choose the correct answer A,B, C, or D. There is one correct answer.

1: A report by a mental health charity shows

A: that nearly 13 million people suffer from stress and anxiety at work.

B: that half of all workers say they suffer from stress and anxiety at work.

C: that nearly 13 million work-days per year are stressful.

D: that stress is good for workforce productivity.

2: Many people who work long hours claim to do so to

A: avoid having a family.

B: escape the stress of family life.

C: earn more money than their co-workers.

D: avoid spending time getting to know their partner.

3: What triggers physiological responses needed for a quick getaway?

A: stress

B: survival of the fittest

C: adrenalin and cortisol

D: the appearance of a dog around the corner

Answer the questions below.
Choose NO MORE THAN THREE WORDS from the passage for each answer.

4: Proteins triggered by bouts of stress in animals have a protective effect and help repair and eliminate cell damage.

What is this cell damage caused by?

_____

5: What are people under stress less likely to react positively to, according to studies?

_____

6: What partly determines how much our tension levels rise?

_____

Complete the summary of paragraph F below.
Choose NO MORE THAN THREE WORDS from the passage for each answer.

The most obvious jobs don't always **7**_____ the most stressful. Saqib Saddiq, who works for recruitment company SHL, revealed that librarians experience **8**_____ than people working for the emergency services. Librarians claimed that their jobs lacked **9**_____ whereas people in what appear to be more stressful jobs were happier and more relaxed. Variety at work is key to job satisfaction and low stress levels, it seems.

Choose the correct answer A,B, C, or D. There is one correct answer.

10: What is an appropriate title for paragraph G?

A: Commuters have it easy

B: Commuting by train

C: The typical commute

D: Commuting – a stressful experience

This reading passage has seven paragraphs, A-G.
Which paragraph contains the following information?

Write the correct letter A-G in the answer section.
NB Not all the paragraphs will be used.

		ANSWER
11:	Although we rarely need the flight or fight response it is useful in some circumstances.	_____
12:	High levels of cortisol generated by stress can have a negative impact on the body.	_____
13:	Fire fighters enjoy the variety in the work they do.	_____
14:	Commuters often feel a sense of helplessness on their journey.	_____

Vocabulary

Vocabulary

A. **Study the text to try to understand the meaning of the words in bold.**

A Dying Continent

At Lakeside College, in one of the poorer **districts** of Kampala, Uganda, a teenage schoolgirl stood up to **recite** a poem. In the dusty classroom, she faced her **peers** and held out her arms to them, almost as an appeal.

"They ate sweets because they are sweet," she intoned. "Then AIDS ate their **flesh**... .What curse brought AIDS to them, the **condemned** generation?"

It's a rhetorical question across 54 countries in Africa - asked by orphans, families, priests, officials and politicians; asked in schools, clinics, parliaments and at gravesides. There seems to be no clear answer. But there is a **sense** of crisis, which is **galvanising** some African governments to make **radical** plans to save their populations in the face of the pandemic. According to UNAIDS, around 26.6 million people in sub-Saharan Africa are living with HIV/ AIDS and the disease has **devastated** families, leaving 11 million children, continent-wide, without parents. During 2011, the average **prevalence** rate across the region was around 8%, but in Botswana and Swaziland it was nearly 40%.

Across the continent there have been varying responses to the HIV/ AIDS pandemic over the past two decades, ranging from **denial** to **pragmatic** acceptance of the disease. The adolescent pupils in Kampala who call themselves the "condemned generation" are in fact the lucky ones, as their government has led the way in AIDS prevention. Uganda is **hailed** as the success story; a country where, against the odds, the people are beating the disease. But what sets Uganda apart from other counties is how **swiftly** its political leaders accepted the reality of the situation.

B. **Complete these sentences with the correct form of one of the words in bold in the text. You will not need to use all the words.**

1. Teenagers are often persuaded to behave badly by their ....

2. We need to do something to .... everybody into action, otherwise the build project will never be completed.

3. There is a real .... of sadness among all the staff at work, since our boss died.

4. If you don't act .... , it will be too late.

5. News of his death .... his whole family.

6. This singer has been .... as the new Elvis Presley.

7. His bones aren't broken; he just has some .... wounds.

8. He has been .... to a life of misery now that he's married that moody woman.

Idioms and Parts of the Body

C. Complete each of the idioms with a suitable form of the words below. Some of the words may be used more than once.

foot	leg	head	face	chest	arm	teeth	finger	eye	hand

1. be on its last ....
2. laugh one's .... off
3. keep one's .... crossed
4. get out of ....
5. keep a straight ....
6. put your .... down
7. see .... to eye with someone
8. put one's .... in it
9. keep a(n) .... on someone
10. get something off your ....
11. pull someone's ....
12. find one's ....
13. cost a(n) .... and a leg
14. be armed to the ....

D. Use a dictionary to find the meanings of the idioms that you are not familiar with. Using some of the idioms in exercise C, think of suitable responses to the statements below.

Suggested answers:

1. You always seem to argue with your sister. _Example: We don't see eye to eye._ _____

2. It's really important that John passes these exams. _____

3. I'm finding it hard to learn how to do my new job. _____

4. Have you seen Jane's new Ferrari? _____

5. George is so funny when he talks about his new girlfriend. _____

6. Can I leave the baby with you for half an hour? _____

7. I wish I could share my problem with someone. _____

8. Jenny told me she is engaged to a Swedish Prince. _____

Reading

CRISIS POINT

The AIDS virus is still the single most potent killer in Sub-Saharan Arica, an area which accounts for just over 10% of the world's population but nearly two-thirds of all **incidents** of the virus. With an average **prevalence** rate of about 7% in the general population and an adult-prevalence rate of one in five, the AIDS crisis has truly reached **epidemic** proportions, or, to put it more correctly, it has become a **pandemic**.

In Botswana, which is in the throes of one of the world's most severe AIDS epidemics, nearly a quarter of all young adults (age 15 – 49) are HIV positive, and most will contract full-blown AIDS due to inadequate medical support and poor sanitation. The disease is more prevalent among young females (age 15 - 24) than young males by a factor of nearly 3 – an alarming statistic considering the fact that it can be passed directly from mother to child during pregnancy. Essential medicines known as AIDS blockers are now being **administered** to pregnant women in a desperate attempt to stem the flow of the disease. In 99% of cases, these blockers are effective; however, they leave behind a very sad legacy – 20% of all births in Botswana now produce AIDS orphans; healthy children whose mothers have **succumbed** to the disease.

Only Swaziland faces a more hopeless **plight**. Here, life expectancy has halved since the turn of the century, a mere decade ago. 64% of all deaths are now AIDS-related, and a staggering 26% of the population is infected. The country is staring into the face of oblivion.

A. Look at the chart below. Decide which label, 1-5, should go with each column, A-E.

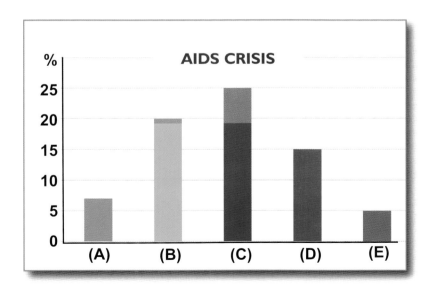

1. Percentage of People infected with AIDS in Sub-Saharan Africa _____
2. Percentage of Young Women in Botswana infected _____
3. Percentage of Young Men in Botswana infected _____
4. Percentage of Young Adults in Botswana infected _____
5. Percentage of the Adult Population of Sub-Saharan Africa infected _____

B. Match the words in bold in the text to their definitions below.

1. given (a drug or medicine) _____

2. disease widespread in one country _____

3. surrender; give in _____

4. struggle (of a people/place) _____

5. incidence; frequency _____

6. cases _____

7. disease widespread in many countries _____

C. Choose four words from the words in bold in the original text to complete this paragraph.

Spanish Flu

Spanish Flu is thought to have originated in America, where it first became a(n)

(1) _____ . It quickly spread across the world - even to the Arctic -

and became the deadliest **(2)** _____ in history. An estimated 50 mil-

lion people **(3)** _____ to the virus. Incidents of the Flu were rarer in

the young and old, and more common in healthy adults, a characteristic rather

unique to this infection as most viruses target those with weakened immunity. The

death toll was made worse by many health agencies recommending aspirin be

(4) _____ in large quantities to patients, resulting in a host of

aspirin-poisoning-related deaths.

Reading - 3

Pre-Reading
A. Think about the questions below. Write short answers and then read the text.

1. How would your life be different if you could not see?

2. How do you think being blind would affect the life of a very poor person living in a third world country?

3. What are your thoughts about the inequality of resources, such as those for medical care, throughout the world?

Reading - 3

And The Blind Shall See

Modified from an article by Geoffrey Tabin, published in The American Alpine Journal, 2002

A The expedition begins with the usual frenzied packing in Kathmandu. Each box is carefully labelled. We double-check all the necessary equipment, as there will be no chance of getting supplies along the way. We fly first to Lhasa and then over spectacular unexplored mountains to land in Xining, in the Tibetan-populated Quinghai Province of China. We proceed in old Chinese jeeps across the rugged landscape of the Amdo region, one of the poorest places in one of the poorest countries in the world.

B Our jeep bounces along a heavily rutted road winding along a high plateau. A few scattered settlements of bare wood and mud **hovels** cling to the steep hillsides **adjacent to** the road. White Buddhist prayer flags flap in the wind on top of each box-like dwelling. Yaks and goats graze on the sparse grass in the brown remnants of barley fields. At nearly 15,000 feet the temperature dips below freezing every night. There is no electricity or even firewood to be found in this region. Cooking is done over open fires of dried yak dung.

C Life is harsh here, particularly if you are blind. And the high Tibetan plateau has one of the highest rates of cataract blindness in the world. The two local doctors whom we brought to Nepal for basic training in cataract surgery have pre-screened patients and tell us that there are more than 300 people in the **county** of about 800 households who are totally blind from cataracts in both eyes.

D Our jeep moves off the **rutted** dirt track and on to the pavement of Golog, the only large settlement for several hundred miles. Many of the buildings are Chinese prefab concrete blocks and most of the officials are Chinese, but the population is over-whelmingly Tibetan nomad. We pull up in front of the county hospital. Our team includes my partner, Dr. Sanduk Ruit, a Nepalese ophthalmologist, two nurses and two technicians from our eye hospital in Kathmandu, plus the two Tibetan doctors, Dr. Wong and Dr. Sangye whom we have been training. Here we will also work with and teach two local nurses and two assistants.

E Dr. Sanduk Ruit is a master surgeon. Ruit trained at the best hospitals in India and then spent two years studying micro-surgery in the Netherlands and Australia. He became the first Nepali doctor to perform modern cataract surgery with a sight restoring lens implant. Previously all doctors in the region sliced the eyeball in half, pulled out the entire lens, sewed the eye shut with crude sutures and gave the patients thick glasses that provided some focus but also a lot of **distortion**. It is not surprising that the second leading cause of blindness in Nepal (after cataract) is bad cataract surgery. Dr. Ruit adapted modern techniques to his environment and perfected high volume delivery of high quality cataract surgery in remote regions at a cost of less than 20 dollars per surgery.

F Rumors of this eye camp began **circulating** in the Golog County several months ago. Hundreds of elderly Tibetans and their families have gathered around the hospital. Their gazes combine a mixture of hope and doubt. No one has ever been cured of blindness here before.

G The hospital has the sickly smell of many such Third World facilities, a mixture of the acrid odor of stale urine with the over-powering scents of excrement and antiseptic. The halls and tables are dusty. Filthy IV tubing and dirty needles litter the hallways. A welcoming committee of flies buzzes in every room. There is no heat. The power is out. As the portable microscopes, generator, and other supplies are unloaded, Dr. Ruit looks across the barren dirt courtyard of the hospital and gives me a broad smile. Pointing at the blind crowd, he excitedly exclaims that everything is perfect.

H Twelve hours per day for the next three days Dr. Ruit and I operate side by side without any high tech equipment beyond a microscope. When the generator fails we keep working on eyes illuminated by assistants holding flashlights. Technicians inject local anaesthetic and prepare the patients for surgery. When a case is finished the patient is rolled off one side of the table as the next patient is rolled on. The face is painted with antiseptic and the surgery continues. The **turnover** time between patients is less than a minute. Dr. Ruit **sustains** a pace of seven perfect surgeries per hour for the 12-hour operating day.

I In nine days a total of 506 cataract surgeries are performed. There are no infections and no blinding **complications**. More importantly, Dr. Wong and Dr. Sangye have each completed more than 75 successful cataract surgeries. We **donate** the microscopes, surgical instruments, and enough lenses for each doctor to **restore** sight to another 500 people. The total cost of the skills transfer including bringing the local doctors to Nepal for training, transporting our team to Golog, buying all the microscopes and surgical instruments to donate, and restoring sight to over 500 eyes is less than $25,000.

J More than 90 percent of the blindness in the world is preventable or treatable. In mountainous Asia, over 70 percent of the blind people can have their vision completely restored with cataract surgery. In Tibet there are no services for the blind. Sightless people require family members to care for them, an enormous economic **burden.** The life expectancy of the blind in this part of the world is less than half that of sighted people the same age. However after surgery most patients can return to work or traditional roles within their family.

First Reading

B. Which paragraph, labelled A-J, contains the following information?

   NB You may use any letter more than once or not at all.

1. how Dr. Ruit changed eye surgery
2. Dr. Ruit's attitude when facing difficulty
3. how the waiting patients were feeling
4. what happened to the equipment after the camp
5. what happens to blind people in Tibet
6. how the team travelled to Lhasa
7. the conditions in the Golan county hospital
8. how many successful surgeries took place
9. how long the surgeons work each day
10. the total cost of the expedition
11. the religion of the local people
12. who went on the expedition

1.	
2.	
3.	
4.	
5.	
6.	
7.	
8.	
9.	
10.	
11.	
1.	

Second Reading

C. Choose the correct answer A, B, C or D to answer the questions.

1. **What is notable about blindness on the Tibetan plateau?**
    A. There is a blind person in every family.
    B. It is unusually common.
    C. Blind people continue with their ordinary lives.
    D. Little is known about the causes.

2. **Most people who live in Golog are**
    A. suffering from cataracts.
    B. Tibetan nomads.
    C. Chinese.
    D. officials and their families.

3. **The hospital in Golog is described as**
    A. the worst ever seen by the surgeons.
    B. welcoming.
    C. in perfect condition.
    D. unsanitary.

4. **The burden of blindness in Tibet**
    A. is mostly unnecessary.
    B. is exclusively economic.
    C. is fairly insignificant.
    D. has been lifted.

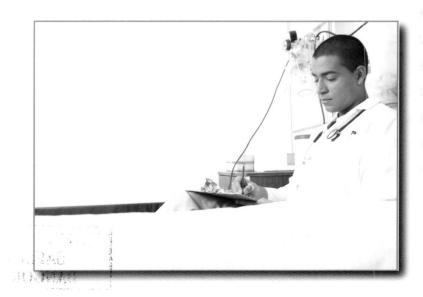

Vocabulary in context

D. Find a word in bold in the text that has the same meaning as (or a similar meaning to) each of the following definitions:

1. uneven due to depressions left by wheels _____

2. beside, neighbouring, next to _____

3. has the effect of continuing something for a period of time _____

4. a change in the appearance or sound which causes something to become unclear _____

5. to give, without charge; to help others _____

6. problems; a medical condition that is due to another illness _____

7. a heavy load that is difficult to carry; something that causes great difficulty _____

8. change; the rate something leaves and is replaced _____

9. small, broken hut; home of the very poor _____

10. moving freely around a place or group _____

11. a region with its own local government _____

12. to bring back to a previous condition _____

E. Use the correct form of the words from Exercise A above to complete the sentences.

1. The old painting was almost unrecognisable after it was .... to its original form.

2. The .... of keeping the secret was more than Amy could bear; she had to tell someone.

3. I could not hear what he was saying because there was so much .... on the telephone line.

4. Tom's running very fast; I doubt that he can .... such speed for the rest of the marathon.

5. Because working conditions are not good, the factory has a very high .... of staff.

6. The surgery was successful and Jane should be back home next week as long as there are no ....

7. This is a quiet flat because it's .... a large park.

8. Even though he was from a neighbouring .... , he lived in such a tiny village that I'd never heard of it.

9. The hills in the nature reserve were deeply .... due to illegal motorcycle racing.

10. They asked the wedding guests to .... to a charity instead of bringing gifts.

11. Tourists rarely leave the resorts or see the .... where most of the local people dwell.

12. The news quickly .... around the whole town.

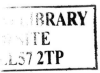